YOUR
NAVIGATOR

YOUR NAVIGATOR

Leadership principles from a military flying career
that will help you to find your way as a leader

Richard Cartlidge

CONTENTS

PROLOGUE

"Per ardua ad astra – through adversity to the stars."
—Motto of the Royal Air Force

I joined the Royal Air Force on the 16th August 1992 and served as a navigator for the next sixteen years. Since leaving the Royal Air Force in 2008 I have continued to be a navigator, developing leadership and supporting leaders to find their own way in a variety of settings.

I have met few people who have had a clear route through life, to end up where they originally expected to. My own journey has had its fair share of detours, wrong turns and surprises. However, I am a firm believer that adversity forges leadership and leaders. I am proud to have served in the Royal Air Force which, in 2018, celebrated its centenary anniversary. In the early days the Royal Air Force was populated by an open-minded, forward looking demographic which reflected the social mobility of the early 20th Century. The paradoxical blend of maverick and convention has characterized leadership in the Royal Air Force, which has a history of challenging the norm whilst championing diversity and inclusion to get the job done. For instance, 18 different nations were represented in the crews who flew and fought in the Battle of Britain.

The Royal Air Force motto states *through* adversity, not avoiding adversity or skirting around adversity. All leaders will face adversity at some point whether it be at a personal level or on an organisational scale. I experienced adversity in different forms throughout my Royal

Air Force career and beyond. As a navigator I have come to recognise some key leadership qualities and I have learnt some valuable principles that have helped me to chart a course through adversity.

This book is my offer to share these with you. What makes a good navigator is someone who can recognise where you are now and help you with a route to where you want to get to. To be honest, technology can increasingly do this for you nowadays. What makes a great navigator is someone who can empathise with where you are and who you are, someone who can truly understand your situation, someone who can think innovatively and contingently about your plan and communicate the way forward in congruent and familiar language. In this book, as your navigator, my intention is to equip you and support you on your own leadership journey – and in doing so enable you to reach your stars.

AUTHOR'S NOTE

I have changed some of the names in this book to protect the identities of friends and colleagues. My anecdotes as told in this book are written from my own personal memory and recollections of the events I experienced. I have done my best to portray them accurately and realistically. Any factual mistakes herein are entirely of my own making.

INTRODUCTION

We'd had a good day on the beach. Sandcastles had been made, balls thrown and caught, paddling and splashing been done in the waves. It was warm and sunny with a steady breeze flapping the flags in the late afternoon. I was putting my son, then three years old, into his car seat having washed the sand off his feet while my wife Sarah was sorting out our 20-month-old daughter, on the other side of the car. I am sure we would discover plenty more Pembrokeshire sand in nappies and pants later, but we made an effort to return what we could to the car park. We were making the most of taking a holiday during term time whilst our children were pre-school age and we had been fortunate with the weather. It was warm and sunny with a gentle on-shore breeze that carried distant noises from the many people still on the beach – happy sounds of screams and yelps as people swam in the surf and played games on the beach. It was time for us to get back to our accommodation for tea before the children became over-tired. The radio was on in the car – BBC Radio 2's Steve Wright in the afternoon show was playing quietly. I wasn't really paying attention as my son and I were chatting about the day, but I noticed that Steve had interrupted the show for a news broadcast. Something was being reported about planes flying into skyscrapers in New York. It was 11th September 2001.

Sarah and I sat in the car and looked at each other. "This sounds bad" Sarah said in a solemn tone. We were both aware that news events like this would have an impact on my work – I was a Royal Air Force Navigator on an operational Chinook Squadron. There was a high likelihood that a military response to such an event could involve me in some way. I looked at our children on the back seat, happily babbling away to each other, blissfully unaware of the catastrophic, world changing event that was unfolding.

Four months later, in early January 2002, I was flying out to Salalah in Oman as a lead crew member of a 27 Squadron Support Helicopter detachment to HMS *Illustrious*. The detachment was embarked, meaning we were based on board the ship as part of the ship's company as it sailed around the Indian Ocean. We were to relieve the first detachment of crews who had been embarked for six weeks since November 2001 and we were to sail with HMS *Illustrious* into the Indian Ocean to await orders. We anticipated that we would be flying into Afghanistan with members of 42 Commando to seek out Osama Bin Laden, flush out the Taliban and play our part in the global response to the history defining event of 9/11.

It's important to highlight that being embarked on a Royal Navy Warship is not something that we as Royal Air Force crews were familiar with. With the exception of a twenty-four-hour deck landing training exercise in the Solent during the previous autumn, which included a night stop on board, I had not experienced life aboard a Royal Navy Ship. It may be easy to the civilian observer to regard the armed forces as all the same. There are different uniforms and hardware, but we are all military, aren't we? Not quite. Whilst there is a common identity regarding duty, service and patriotism, in reality, there are vast differences between the Royal Navy, The British Army and the Royal Air Force; each has its own unique culture and sub-culture. Perhaps it is obvious to say but the Royal Navy are focussed on being aboard ships and their training from day one is oriented around this. It was quite strange for my personal navigational orientation to go to sleep at one latitude and longitude and wake up somewhere different – especially when the view outside was the same monochromatic ocean. The environment, culture and routine were all new to me. There was no airfield with wildlife and grass and space; all around us was metallic and man-made. There was a constant, twenty-four seven noise from the engines and generators that powered the ship. There was regular close contact with the Ship's company in the corridors who busily made their way around the ship carrying out their duties. There always seemed to be something happening, such as drills to practice responding to incidents like fires or flooding; there was maintenance work on some part of the ship or briefings and orders being transmitted through the ships tannoy. The Ship was a busy, active, non-stop community and we had to integrate quickly, as well as pull our own weight and contribute to the regular duties on board. There is an adage that the Royal Navy has traditions, the Army has customs and the Royal Air Force has habits. In the Royal Air Force, we were the Junior Service, and we were on board a ship of the Senior Service – their flagship no less. We would need to work hard to win the respect of our hosts through professionalism and collaboration to make sure that we were not regarded as an intrusive, immature cousin.

The day before we sailed from Salalah we received some orientation briefings. As part of my familiarisation with the ship I found myself on the bridge. I noticed a Commander there - a quiet and reserved man. We exchanged pleasantries and acknowledged our respective roles – he was the ship's navigator; I was a Royal Air Force navigator.

I reflected on both my role as navigator and the role of the Ship's navigator on HMS *Illustrious*. Here was a warship that represented our nation. She[1] was the flagship for the Royal Navy. She was a tool for politicians to project foreign policy. She could be stationed off-shore as a military presence ready to deploy military hardware into war zones, as was the reason for me being there. She could be sent to disaster zones to provide humanitarian relief. She was much smaller in terms of crew size and displacement than comparable ships from allied Navies, but HMS *Illustrious* had a formidable presence and an esteemed pedigree. I remembered her from her involvement in The Falkland's Conflict in 1982, for instance. She represented more than the embarked personnel or military hardware that she carried. She represented the purpose, identity, beliefs and values of a nation. This amazing capability was under the direction of the current captain and delivered by a well-trained and motivated crew. And yet I was, and I am still intrigued by the navigator role. Without navigation all of that capability and representation would be flawed...even with modern and cutting-edge technology, ships including the Royal Navy's, run into peril and occasionally run aground due to human navigational error. Good navigation would make sure that this wonderful ship would be where it needed to be; would travel safely to its destinations and ultimately deliver on its purpose. Leaders, like ships, can benefit from a good navigator to get to where they need to be and to deliver what they are capable of.

The modern world has arguably made navigation easy for us, so much so that we can take it for granted. Most cars have satellite navigations systems that we can blindly believe and follow – with no awareness of how they work or what they are actually doing. We embark on journeys in life but may not know exactly where we are

---

[1] I've often wondered why ships are referred to with great endearment in the female gender. The best reason I have heard is it is because they carry people...as women do. Accordingly, they need our respect and care.

starting from or what our actual destination is; so how on earth will we know when we've got there? In the same way that we have abdicated our responsibility for journey planning and guidance to automated, impersonal machines so too we can journey through life without regarding where we are starting from, not considering what's going on in our current environment that is enabling or hindering the journey, and not looking ahead to see where we could actually get to with a little courage and ambition.

We need navigators in life to tell us where we are and to help us to get to where we want to go. People are drawn to causes, something that aligns and connects with their beliefs, passions and values – much like HMS *Illustrious* represented the beliefs, passions and values of a nation. The context may be in the workplace, or it may be outside of work; but people like to follow causes. So, when an environment is created that empowers people to contribute to 'their' cause it can unlock tremendous energy and potential for brilliant results to be realised. The architects of causes are leaders, people with the ability to apply their unlimited talent to the cause and somehow make the cause compelling for others to follow. So how do leaders know the way?

I have had the opportunity to work with talented leaders in a variety of settings, including organisationally, in teams and one on one. I want to share with you some of the thinking, tools and techniques that in my experience so far have unlocked potential and realised leadership. I will resist the temptation to be 'absolute' in my approach; I don't believe there is a silver bullet or a 'top 10', 'top 5' or even 'top 3' list of things that will guarantee success. I firmly believe that we all have the potential to be brilliant. I want to be your navigator and offer guidance and support on your leadership journey to being brilliant.

Ultimately, we are all on a journey called life. Within that journey are multiple other journeys: family, career, relationships, projects, illnesses and so on. Within your journey you are a leader. Your current episode may involve leading a corporate body of several thousand people or it could be a relationship with one person. If you have the opportunity to relate and influence, then you have the opportunity to be a leader. I will heighten your self-awareness of where you are on your journey, give you some guidance on planning how to progress and highlight hazards that may get in the way. It's your journey and it's your life – you are responsible for success or failure. However, often a bit of encouragement can go a long way in making progress.

Embarked on HMS *Illustrious* I experienced fear, uncertainty, excitement, fun and fulfilment. I knew the ultimate destination for the mission, Afghanistan. I didn't know when I embarked exactly what the journey would look and feel like. However, as a navigator I had experiences and skill that equipped me to achieve the mission. This book is my contribution that I hope will serve your leadership journey.

How this book works:

Each chapter has two parts. The first part is a personal anecdote of an experience that has formed my view of a leadership quality or principle. The second part of the chapter is to encourage you to transfer this quality or principle to your own context. Finally, each chapter has some provocative questions from your navigator aimed at helping you to think through aspects of your current leadership journey and present you with a call to action.

The chapters cover my personal view of what constitutes primary leadership qualities and key leadership principles. Each of these has been drawn from my own experiences and interpretations in a variety of settings. My intention is never to tell you how to be a leader in your own context. Rather, I offer you the tools that I have found are consistently needed in any leadership scenario; that you may be able to apply them for yourself and realise the results.

From the sub-zero winter of Bosnia to the stifling summer heat of Kosovo; visiting an 18th Century English carpenter, a spring invasion of Afghanistan and sharing experiences of the British military's officer and aircrew training world; I hope you will enjoy a journey that intends to enhance your understanding and practice of your own leadership as you travel with your navigator.

Welcome aboard!

---

navigator / 'navigerte/ *n.* **1** *a person skilled in or engaged in navigation.*

A **navigator** *is the person on board a ship or aircraft responsible for its navigation. The navigator's primary responsibility is to be aware of ship or aircraft position at all times. Responsibilities include planning the journey, advising the captain or commander of estimated timing to destinations while en route, and ensuring hazards are avoided.*

LEADERSHIP QUALITIES

HUMILITY

*"The first responsibility of a leader is to define reality.
The last is to say thank you. In between the two,
the leader must become a servant."*
—Max De Pree

*"Humility is not thinking less of yourself;
it is thinking of yourself less."*
—Rick Warren

"Humble service is the heart of true power."
—Justin Welby

*"If you're the smartest person in the room,
you're in the wrong room."*
—Confucius

*"The X Factor of great leadership is not personality,
it's humility."*
—Jim Collins

In the weeks after 9/11 there was a new world order responding to the murderous events in New York. Our Squadron had been participating in a large desert operations training exercise in Oman through August and September 2002. Instead of all the airframes (helicopters) coming home it was decided that two would embark on *HMS Illustrious* and be available for Operations in the

Middle East and beyond. My detachment replaced the first wave of crews in January 2002 and by March the likelihood of flying into Afghanistan in support of 42 Commando was imminent.

By March 2002 our detachment of aircrew and engineers from 27 Squadron, along with two embarked Chinook helicopters, had been on board Royal Navy warships for ten weeks – despite being scheduled to do only a six-week detachment. After the initial days of familiarising ourselves with the ship's environment and routines we quickly got into the familiar military practice of waiting. It is easy to highlight the exciting things that happen in the military but in reality, a lot of time on exercises and operations is spent waiting. To be fair this time can useful for training for the crews for a specific event that is expected to happen. There is kit to be prepared, intelligence to be understood and planning for various scenarios. It is also important to respect that behind the scenes many people work hard to ensure that the political conditions are right for any forthcoming military action. Nevertheless, the nature of military life can be that there are long periods waiting for the optimum conditions for a mission to take place. We knew we would be heading for Afghanistan, but the specifics of how and when were not yet known.

For the first six weeks of our detachment we were aboard HMS *Illustrious* and then we transferred to HMS *Ocean*. Most of that time had been spent sailing in racetracks in the Indian Ocean but we did have some interesting excursions to Bahrain and Oman as well as some unique experiences. On one occasion five aircraft carriers and their respective support ships from four different NATO nations assembled in close proximity to make a spectacular photo shoot; HMS Illustrious took centre stage but was admittedly dwarfed by her American, French and Italian counterparts. On my mum's birthday I called her via satellite phone to wish her a happy birthday – much to her surprise as we were regularly out of communications with loved ones. The best experience for me though was on my own 32nd birthday – we had been tasked to transport some passengers between HMS *Illustrious* and the *USS John C. Stennis*. As someone who was 16 when the movie 'Top Gun' was released having the opportunity to get up close and personal to an American nuclear-powered aircraft carrier was not to be missed. We were not allowed to shut down on deck since it was effectively an active airfield where space was precious – and if we couldn't have restarted our airframe would literally have been pushed over the side. This wouldn't have proven popular with the British taxpayer. So we landed, disembarked our passengers and then requested to hover in the 'starboard wait'[2] to watch the *USS John C. Stennis* launch and recover her air wing: F-14s and F-18s taking off and landing using the full deck space - a true scene from 'Top Gun' and a privilege to watch for 20 minutes or so. And when it was over, I did request a fly by and we did complete a low-level fly past below deck height, much to the appreciation of the deck crew.

Despite all of these 'jollies' the time was approaching when we would need to do what we had been sent out to do, which was fly into Afghanistan. The orders came on 26th March 2002. We were to launch in the early hours at 0200 local time, in darkness, fly at high altitude of about 8,000 feet over Pakistan and time our arrival at

---

[2] Helicopters, by virtue of their ability to take off and land vertically (and not necessarily requiring a runaway) are often provided with procedures to arrive and depart from airfields perpendicular to the main approach (runway) direction. The Starboard Wait is a holding area right of the centreline of the ship as one faces forward which is clear of the extended approach and take-off paths of the runway for fixed wing aircraft. Helicopters would hold in this position until cleared to land on deck.

Kandahar for first light. Following a refuelling stop we would then progress at low level, less than one hundred feet above ground level, through Afghanistan to Kabul and land at Bagram air base. I had been selected for this detachment as a QHTI, meaning a Qualified Helicopter Tactics Instructor, and for my longevity and experience on the Squadron. I had been serving on Chinook Squadrons for over six years at this point and I was at the top of my game – all of my training was put into practice: I led the full mission planning cycle which was a comprehensive preparation for the mission ahead of us. We completed a series of thorough briefings that covered everything from weather and what equipment our aircraft had through to intelligence updates and what we would do if we were forced to land, either through technical malfunction or enemy action. We assembled our kit which included our personal belongings – we were effectively moving home – and our personal weapons. The latter always reminded me of the significance of what we were doing and the responsibility that came with carrying guns and bullets. I was always mindful that each round in my magazine could take a life. It was a sobering thought and made everything feel serious. We were flying into a war zone where there were people who, given the opportunity, would cause us grievous harm.

We were ready to go. All of the staff officers on board came to personally wish us the traditional 'Godspeed' farewell. Their best wishes were welcome although in a way I felt a little like they were conveying their own anxiety for the uncertainty of what lay ahead of us. In some ways most of what we were doing was very familiar and very routine, we had all flown together before on operations in Northern Ireland, Bosnia and Kosovo. However, this time it was a one-way trip, we would not be returning to our take off point. *HMS Ocean* would position us as close to the coast as possible to reduce our flying time and once we were airborne she would be heading south west and back to other duties, having played her part in the wider mission to deliver aircraft and Royal Marines to the theatre of war. So once we were airborne there was a limited window of opportunity to return to deck before we would be out of range of each other and we would be on our own.

Shortly before 0200hrs we walked onto the darkened deck of *HMS Ocean* under a moonless, cloudless sky towards the silhouettes of our aircraft. We boarded the aircraft, strapped in and started up. Soon the dark night was filled with the noise of two CH-47 Chinook helicopters beating their rotas with their characteristic 'wokka' signature sound. The commandos and engineers were signalled to board and once they were strapped in we prepared to launch. At 0200hrs the two Chinooks lifted into the black night and we bid farewell to our ten-week nautical home.

There was a subdued mood among the crew. We all knew our roles and the task ahead. We were also aware of the seriousness of the situation. All of us had flown in Bosnia and were aware of the bloody brutality in the Balkan region's recent history - the reason we had been deployed there was to act as peace-keeping and stabilising forces. However, now we were entering Afghanistan where the mission was different – and the mountains were bigger and the enemy, from what our intelligence told us, was even nastier. The Combat Search and Rescue[3] part of our briefing, specifically what would happen to us if we were captured by the Taliban, was grim. We knew that an American helicopter had been shot down in the

---

[3] Combat Search and Rescue – the plan of action for the crew and passengers in the event that the helicopter was forced down in enemy territory by either mechanical fault or enemy action.

previous weeks up country and the outcome for those on board at the hands of the Taliban was gruesome. There was a degree of anxiety regarding the unknown ahead of us. However, this was coupled with a resolve to get the job done – none of us were there by accident. I had come to realise that one of the defining aspects of being in the operational side of the military is that we put ourselves in harm's way in order to achieve something for the greater good. There was a big picture here; and we had a small part to play in it.

We got airborne and soon established ourselves at altitude and on track. There were multiple checks and procedures that needed to be carried out both inside the aircraft – arming weapons and settling into the Night Vision Goggle (NVG) flying routine - through to communications and checks for joining the Composite Air Operation (COMAO) using standard NATO procedures. As the navigator this was a busy period for me in the dim green light of the cockpit. The airspace over Afghanistan was understandably tightly controlled by allied, primarily American, forces. An aircraft, military or civilian, could not just fly through the airspace and to be frank they wouldn't want to. A lot of ordnance – bullets and missiles - was constantly airborne and strapped to fighter jets to ensure that air superiority was maintained. Therefore, we had to check into the airspace and identify ourselves as friendly in order to proceed with the mission.

To do this we needed to speak to the Airborne Warning and Control System (AWACS). The AWACS is a 24/7 presence that monitors and controls the airspace in operational theatres through a fleet of Boeing E-3 Sentry aircraft – recognisable by their large rotating radar disc that sits on top of the aircraft. The operators on board the AWACS were monitoring a large area of airspace and so there needed to be a way of identifying our location to the AWACS so that they could confirm whether we were friend or foe and subsequently track our mission, ensuring it corresponded with the mission details they had for us. This was a comforting thought, to know that if we got into difficulty either through enemy action or some malfunction we could call on support instantly. We identified our position to the AWACS using a bullseye protocol. All forces participating in the COMAO would be briefed on the location of a bullseye – an arbitrary and secret latitude and longitude that could be referenced by bearing and distance to inform other assets of a position. I needed to contact AWACS on the designated frequency, identify ourselves to them and confirm our position so that it was safe to proceed with the mission.

Having said farewell to *HMS Ocean* I dialled up the frequency for AWACS and made my call, his callsign was Magic:

"Magic this is Vortex airborne as fragged[4], we are bullseye 160 degrees 80 nautical miles, requesting a parrot and India check."

Vortex was our callsign. Fragged told the AWACS that we were on the COMAO mission list and what our mission was, and a parrot and India check was the invitation to the AWACS to use some of their equipment to interrogate some equipment on our aircraft that would confirm our identity.

"Good morning Vortex, stand by," replied the AWACS operator.

There was a pause whilst the operator looked for us on his radar in the area we had referenced through bullseye and he would then call us back.

"Vortex this is Magic, nothing seen."

Hmmm. *"Nothing seen"* meant that he hadn't seen us on his radar

---

[4] A fragmentory order is an abbreviated form of an operation order usually issued on a day-to-day basis that eliminates the need for restating information contained in a basic operation order. The frag sheet would contain the details of our mission, hence we were operating 'as fragged'.

scope and therefore he couldn't identify us. This was unusual but sometimes happened and required a second attempt. I called back repeating my request.

"Magic, this is Vortex, we are bullseye 160 degrees 80 nautical miles, requesting parrot and India check."

"Roger Vortex, standby."

"Why couldn't he identify us?" I thought. I had carried out this procedure dozens if not hundreds of times before in Bosnia, Kosovo and on numerous training sorties. I was beginning to feel apprehensive, like when you know things are about to go wrong - and all of a sudden time appears to speed up and pressure builds exponentially. When things go wrong in dynamic situations they tend to accelerate unless they can quickly be corrected.

"Vortex, this is Magic, nothing seen."

Damn!

"What's happening Rich?" asked my pilot, who understandably was as perturbed as I was that we were not identified, recognised, and safely established en-route.

"I'm not sure," I said, racking my brain. We had to get this sorted - fast. It was dark in the cockpit and even darker outside. To the naked eye all that could be seen was stars. However, we were flying with Night Vision Goggles attached to our helmets and through the goggles, which amplified light sources, I could see multiple flashing lights high in the sky above us. These were 'black' strobe lights from other aircraft in the AOR[5] operating on infra-red, not visible to the

---

[5] Area of Responsibility (AOR) is a pre-defined geographic region assigned to Combatant commanders that are used to define an area with specific geographic boundaries where they have the authority to plan and conduct operations. For example, during a quiz night in the Wardroom of HMS Ocean that I organised with my fellow RAF colleagues (to ease the boredom and improve morale and collaboration between embarked forces) one of the light-hearted questions was: Q. What is Postman Pat's AOR? A. Greendale.

naked eye; one of them could have been our AWACS - although they were a long way separated from us by distance and altitude. More ominously I knew that out there would be a CAP – a Combat Air Patrol. This would be two or more fighter aircraft that were armed and patrolling, ready to intercept and if necessary, shoot down unauthorised aircraft.

The consequences of at best mis-communication with the AWACS and at worst not being recognised and identified could be severe. Let me briefly take you back to an incident eight years earlier. On 14th April 1994 two US Army UH-60 Black Hawk helicopters were shot down by two US Air Force F-15C Eagle Fighters. Twenty-six people were killed. This happened in daylight, in good flying conditions and following a cease fire in hostilities. Even when procedures were followed, and conditions were favourable, tragedies could happen. We were flying at night, on an operational mission, in the early stages of a military campaign and heading towards one of the most volatile regions on the planet at that time. This was real, and I felt the pressure of the situation – it felt like I was in a dark room and the expectations of both crews on two helicopters were all bearing down on me to get this fixed.

"Maybe they do it the other way around," I thought to myself. This was ludicrous – I knew how to give a bearing and distance relative to bullseye to establish my position. It was a NATO procedure that I was well trained in. But *what if*…what if the operator is looking in the reciprocal airspace? What if instead of looking for our callsign's radar signature on his radar scope at the bearing and distance *from* Bullseye he was actually looking for us as a bearing and distance *to* Bullseye? This would be a completely different piece of airspace hundreds of miles from where we actually were. I did the quick mental maths to calculate the reciprocal bearing and distance from Bullseye and without warning the crew I gave it a try.

"Magic this is Vortex, we are bullseye 340 degrees 80 nautical miles, requesting parrots and India check."

"Roger Vortex, standby."

I was impressed at the lack of impatience or frustration expressed by this guy...with sound professionalism he kept responding to my request with his gentle American accent even though we'd had two failed attempts. It was like we were getting to know each other.

"Vortex this is Magic; your parrots and India are sweet-sweet; welcome to the war!"

Wtf had just happened. Despite being highly trained and fluent with NATO procedures to operate in a war zone, I just had to leave my comfort zone at the start of the mission and do things differently to get the job done.

We had established ourselves in 'Operation Enduring Freedom' and would continue flying our mission to Bagram Airfield, near to the capital of Afghanistan, Kabul. On arrival we were met by our squadron commander, who pointed out two things. First, that the area adjacent to the landing apron was a minefield *"so watch your step!"* he said. Second, that what we had just achieved – flying the first operational Chinook helicopters into Afghanistan after 9/11, launched from a Royal Navy ship – was a significant accomplishment and a demonstration of capability by us as crews and the Support Helicopter Force. We made our way to some rudimentary tented accommodation and, feeling tired from the mission, crashed out on some camp beds.

* * *

It's not about you.

Something in the psyche may 'jar' with this statement when considering leadership. Surely leadership is about standing at the front, being recognised and leading the way no less? Certainly, on the right occasion there is a need for leaders to have presence and to be able to communicate vision and direction. But ego can get in the way of great leadership. In my experience, humility is the more powerful and effective leadership quality. Leadership is about relationship between the leader and their followers. The key to humility is thinking about other people more than we think about ourselves; and for this it is my favourite leadership quality, although I fear it is also rare.

Why is humility my *favourite* leadership quality? Let me unpack this a little. The root of the word humility comes from humus, meaning the organic component of soil, formed by the decomposition of leaves and other plant material by soil microorganisms. In his book 'Prayer', Richard Foster says: *"The word itself comes from the Latin humus, which means fertile ground."* There is something about the ground, or being grounded; and being fertile. The best leaders are, in my view, grounded in the reality and the truth of the context. They do not shy away from what is uncomfortable – they are real. Furthermore, they recognise the value of others around them as a fertile source of contribution. With humility, the leader can first engage with and then benefit from the wisdom and insight of those around them, where ideas and plans may be better than what they could have devised them self. And herein lies the opportunity for empowerment. Peter Hawkins describes leadership as a relational phenomenon - it is about the relationship between the leader and the followers as much as it is about the leader. Great leaders seem to be able to relate incredibly well to their followers and nurture within them engagement and commitment - which in turn unleashes the follower's personal power to address the situation at hand. Richard Foster again:

> *"…put in simple terms, humility means to live as close to the truth as possible: the truth about ourselves, the truth about others, the truth about the world in which we live. It does not mean grovelling or finding the worst possible things to say about ourselves… humility is in fact filled with power to bring forth life."*

The obstacle to humility is ego. If I have ten people in my team and they do a great job, then a part of me wants to take some (or all) of the credit. The opportunity for recognition is seductive, stroking our need to belong. However, with humility I can recognise that they, the followers, are the ones who deserve the recognition; and as leader I need to make sure that they get it.

And it's even more important than that. There is much to be gained by the leader who can practice humility. I worked for several years at The Environment Agency for England and Wales which employed, at the time, twelve thousand people. If you asked me to find a solution for climate change – whatever that means but; by any definition a complicated problem - I could probably give you a very naïve, ill-thought through idea. But if I could engage with 12,000 highly educated, focused people who understood the environmental challenges of our time, then somewhere amongst them would be some very credible ideas – and one of those ideas would be the best one for the reality of the situation. And it probably wouldn't be my idea. Imagine if you could then engage the environmental community globally? Think about the quality of ideas that then would be generated.

The leader who demonstrates and practices humility can be aware of what others have to offer along with recognising their own limitations. This can open the doorway to accepting others' support, perhaps recognising that others have skills more suited to the task. By engaging with them purposefully the leader enables others to contribute what they have to the cause and the leader can ensure that the followers take the recognition.

> *"When the best leader's work is done,*
> *the people say, 'we did it ourselves.'"*
> **—Lao Tzu 6th C**

On that moon-less night on the 26th of March 2002 I had to think about my fellow airman in the AWACS. What was he thinking? What did he need from me so that my mission could progress; and so that he could do his job? Only in answering those questions could I continue with my mission and contribute my small part to a big war.

Questions for you from your navigator.

If humility is more about them than you, then:

- Who else could contribute to the challenge you're facing right now?
- What can you do to engage them with your mission?
- How easy is it for you to give others recognition and, if necessary, the glory?

COURAGE

'Keep your fears to yourself but share your courage with others.'
—**Robert Louis Stevenson**

In 2008 my sixteen-year career in the Royal Air Force was drawing to a close. As with most service leavers I underwent some career transition workshops – activities that aim to support service leavers in their transition to civilian life. These workshops offer a variety of experiences to help service leavers find their next paid job or vocation and help with practical skills such as refreshing, or maybe writing from scratch, a CV. Being in this phase of transition from military back to civilian life prompts reflections. During this time, I remember asking myself: *"when were you at your happiest and most fulfilled?"* My mind raced back to a time before I was even in the Royal Air Force when I was kayaking at Symond's Yat in Herefordshire on the River Wye. I remember being with a group as an instructor and demonstrating to people how to ferry-glide, break-in, break-out and paddle up the white-water rapids. I could hear myself shouting encouragement across the noise of the rushing water to fellow paddlers who were achieving something they didn't think they could do. And that was the thing – I was encouraging people.

It may sound like a soft thing – encouraging people. A simple pat on the back and saying, 'well done'? However, some years after leaving the Royal Air Force my friend Tom helped me to understand what was really going on with encouragement. Breaking down the word to its roots the word encourage is actually *en-courage* - to *impart* courage.

Then the word courage has its root in the French *'le Coeur'* or if you prefer Latin *cor* meaning the heart, for example Richard Coeur de Lyon – Richard the Lion Heart (the King...not me). It became evident to me that to encourage people was to engage with their heart – that mysterious, essential, emotional and powerful organ in the body – and to engage with the passion and drive that could come from it to achieve unprecedented results. Some studies even suggest that the heart has its own intelligence and so enabling that intelligence could truly help leaders to realise their full potential. I realised that I like to encourage people because it challenges them positively to engage with their passions and beliefs; it encourages them to be courageous. And therefore, courage is my second favourite leadership quality after humility.

Kosovo 1999

Throughout the 1990s my time on the Chinook Squadrons ran parallel to ongoing political unrest in the Balkans. Regularly there would be news reports of atrocities and armed uprisings in the area formerly known as Yugoslavia. As I completed my conversion training in the summer of 1995, my final training course before joining an operational Royal Air Force Squadron, Chinook crews were deployed to Ploce in southern Croatia as the first wave of a peace-keeping force to the region. For the next six years a detachment of the Royal Air Force Chinook Support Helicopter Force was deployed to Croatia from where flying operations into Bosnia as part of IFOR[6] and SFOR[7] were mounted. I had been part of several of those detachments. In June 1998 I started my second

---

[6] IFOR: Implementation Force – a NATO-led multinational peace enforcement force in Bosnia and Herzegovina in 1995-1996.
[7] SFOR: Stabilisation Force – a NATO-led multinational peacekeeping force deployed to Bosnia and Herzegovina after the Bosnian war.

operational squadron tour on the newly re-formed operations flight on 27 Sqn where, incidentally, I was led by the best leader I have ever served.

Whilst the detachments to Croatia had become routine and arguably benign, the situation in Kosovo to the south was becoming more volatile. Since 1989 ethnic Albanians in Kosovo had pursued a policy of nonviolent protest against the Serbian president, Slobodan Milosevic for his rejection of the province's constitutional autonomy. Kosovo was an area held sacred to the Serbs and Milosevic objected to the area being under the control of Muslim Albanians. The international community refused to address the issue and a more radical group, the Kosovo Liberation Army (KLA), emerged in 1996. The KLA carried out attacks on Serbian Police and politicians. By 1998 the KLA was considered an armed uprising which led to Serbian special police and Yugoslav armed forces attempts to reassert control over the region. Events escalated, and atrocities were committed by the police, paramilitary groups and the army which culminated in a programme of ethnic cleansing and the consequence that hundreds of thousands of refugees fled the area. After a period of failed diplomatic negotiations, NATO began air strikes on Belgrade in March 1999 and by June NATO and Yugoslavia had signed a peace accord which outlined troop withdrawal and the return of ethnic Albanians to Kosovo. 27 Sqn was to be part of the peace keeping force and in May 1999 we were on our way as part of a seven strong Chinook detachment flying to Macedonia to be based in Skopje, just south of the Kosovan border.

The journey to Macedonia was not without incident. Deployments to distant operations or exercises often meant the Chinooks would be ferried by ship or by heavy cargo airlift aircraft such as Antonov transporters and later on Royal Air Force C-17 aircraft. However, within Europe Chinooks could fly to their destinations. So, to get to Kosovo from the UK we flew south over France, turned east across the Mediterranean and Italy, across the Adriatic, over Albania and into Macedonia. The transit included a refuelling stop in Nice, Southern France. One of the aircraft went unserviceable there and so the crew had an unplanned but not uncomfortable few days on the Cote d'Azur while they waited to get the aircraft fixed. While this sounds very appealing, the truth is that when there is an operational task the crews want to get to the destination and get the job done.

The remaining aircraft were flying in pairs a day or so apart. I was on the second wave. The first wave had arrived in Macedonia. Now, be mindful that this was 1999 and mobile phones were not as prolific or 'smart' as they are today. Notwithstanding, many of the crews had mobile phones and were familiar with texting. As we approached the Albanian border, crossing the Adriatic, we knew there may be uncertainty regarding comms, like who to contact and on what frequency for air traffic control. Fortunately, our colleagues ahead of us were texting back frequencies and protocols for crossing Albanian airspace and arriving in Macedonia. Using non-standard equipment on board Royal Air Force aircraft was prohibited. Even today when flying on commercial aircraft texting is not allowed from boarding to landing. I thought it bizarre that towards the turn of the century when we were professional aviators at the top of our game, drilled in strict protocols on how to operate, we could find ourselves flying into the unknown relying on 'uncleared' kit – our own mobile phones - to access key information to complete the mission. Bizarre, but also recognition of the innovative nature of colleagues to get the job done by whatever means and, when necessary, circumnavigating the rules.

We initially stayed a few nights at a barracks near the town of Prilep. I remember walking into the dormitory where the crews were staying after dinner hoping to see crew mates and engage in some benign activities to pass the time like playing cards together. This was usually a good way to unwind and share some banter; we were limited to how much alcohol we could drink – if any - due to the nature of what we were doing. Usually there was a 'two can' rule, meaning we could drink no more than two cans of beer per evening if we were off duty. A lot of being on operations is about waiting around for something, or *the* thing, to happen. I went to the dormitory where our crews were assigned to sleep; to my surprise as I walked in, I could see that everyone was sat on the end of their bed texting…the mobile phone age had truly arrived. In the absence of any social interaction, I headed out into the warm spring evening to see who else was about. We each had an allowance of a specific number of minutes to use company phones to phone loved ones. I sought out one of the phones from our operations clerk and thought I'd give Sarah a call at home. It was lovely to hear her voice and chat about how things were.

It was easy to forget how stressful life could be for Sarah. I was doing what I was paid to do, what I joined up to do and within reason I knew what was going to happen. Sarah was at home coping alone with an 18-month-old baby at the time, our extended families hundreds of miles away from where we lived, and a paucity of information about how things were with my operational detachment. In later years I would realise how much anxiety and stress Sarah had carried in our relationship with the regular uncertainty about my welfare when I was away from home serving overseas. My job was, after all, dangerous. But on this occasion when I heard her voice, I could tell that Sarah was in an excited mood. She had carried out a pregnancy test and it was positive…we were going to have our second child. I wanted to tell everyone and rush home to celebrate with her. However, I was in Macedonia and we were imminently due to be part of a peace keeping force entering a geography that had experienced horrendous and evil ethnic cleansing and atrocities. I confided in one friend on the Sqn and we had a celebratory beer together, one of our two cans for the evening.

A few days later we relocated to Skopje airport in Macedonia. As is often the case with Support Helicopters there was initially little infrastructure in place to support us. We put up tents within yards of the runway - which was less than ideal given the 24/7 nature of NATO forces flying in and out with supplies around the clock – and we made our temporary home.

For the next few days our daily routine would be to wake before sunrise, have breakfast and carry out a general crew briefing so that we could be available and flexible to launch as incoming tasking required. We would sit around the aircraft ready to go, waiting to see what information our Flight Commander, Mike, would bring on return from his high-level briefing. Usually, Mike would walk back from the briefing tent toward us, his flight crews, who were sat around the aircraft waiting for orders. One of the crewmen, Rob – often smoking a tab - would keep a lookout for him from near the rear of the fuselage of the Chinook closest to the Operations tent. The crews would be sheltering from the strengthening sun in the relative cool of the Chinook's cabin, lounging on the bench seating. As Mike crossed the grassy area between our flight line and the operations tent, we would ask Rob *"any sign?"* and Rob would respond. Sometimes Mike would be walking, head down and looking focussed; *"bad news"* Rob would say. This usually meant there was no flying, or some other nuisance bureaucracy would be the order of the day. Other times Mike would be walking a bit more briskly with his head up and smiling; *"good news"* Rob would say. This usually meant that at least some of us would have some tasking to go and do some flying. We had got into the habit of periodically calling to Rob *"good news or bad news Rob?"* However, on one occasion, at around the time that the end of the senior briefing would be concluding, one of us called out: *"Rob, good news or bad news?"* expecting the usual *"he's heads up"* or *"he's heads down"* response. *"Fuck that…"* Rob exclaimed, hurriedly extinguishing his cigarette and launching into action, *"he's running!"* We all jumped up and quickly got our kit on ready for flying, anticipating that some urgent tasking was imminent – sure enough, Mike wanted us all airborne as soon as possible.

With the minimal brief and a grid reference shared between the crews we got airborne and flew for ten minutes to a large wheat field that was right up against the border with Kosovo. We knew that the NATO forces, led by the British Parachute Regiment and Gurkhas, would be entering Kosovo as a peace-keeping force and liberating it from Serbian control to allow the refugees – several thousand of whom were camped on the northern Macedonian border – back into the country. Only tarmac roads could be used for transport as the widespread threat that minefields had been sown on softer tracks was a real concern. Our task was to transport the Paras and Gurkhas north into Kosovo along Route 65 to Kacanik and eventually Pristina, dropping them off in a leap frog fashion at road bridges which were the only sites that were cleared and which we could be reasonably confident weren't sabotaged. From there the route would be secured and the country would be liberated. However, it was unknown what the intentions of the Serbian Forces were and exactly where they were located. Resistance to the peace keeping liberation meant that we could be met with force – and that meant significantly experienced and sophisticated ex-Soviet anti-aircraft equipment and potentially hostile ground forces. A lot of our routine training was based on the threat from Soviet weapons systems, partially a legacy of decades of Cold War experience and partially due to the proliferation of Soviet equipment to adversaries. The thought of coming face to face with hostile, live Soviet weaponry was unsettling and focussed our minds on our own tactics and defence systems.

In our wheat field, which was swelteringly hot in mid-June, we became aware that despite the initial rush of activity, plans to 'invade' were on hold. It was evident from the discussion taking place around General Sir Mike Jackson, a few yards from where the Chinooks had landed, that extreme caution due to the political volatility of the situation was required and we were on pause. As we were waiting, our detachment intelligence officer thought it would be a good idea to update us on the capabilities of the potentially opposing forces that may be waiting for us. It was a fairly grim briefing to around 30 sweating aircrew crammed into the cabin of one of the Chinooks which felt like a hot oven. We were told of all the different ways that we could be shot down, like missiles, bullets and Rocket Propelled Grenades. The brief ended with an overly and unnecessarily dramatic statement from the junior intelligence officer:

"Remember guys, it only takes one bullet."

There was a pause.

"Thanks a bunch Susie!" remarked our crewman leader in his characteristically surly tone. Needless to say, that brief was over. I realised then that good leadership required emotional intelligence – empathy with the crews involved to demonstrate an understanding of what they we were facing. Our Intelligence Officer was on a different wavelength.

Soon after we were told that we would not be entering Kosovo that day. Interventions at the highest levels in European government had reached an agreement that the Serbian forces would be given 24 hours to withdraw. I often think that had we flown into Kosovo that day we would have been met with significant opposition either by intent or malice, which could have triggered who knows what consequences. However, once again I was reminded that although front line aircrew and troops are the ones who put themselves in harm's way, there is a much bigger team in the military and political hierarchy that work hard to achieve good outcomes – and for that we were grateful. The next day, 12th June 1999, we inserted 5 Airborne Brigade into Kosovo with no mishaps and with no opposition - and thousands of cheering refugees streamed north across the border. Back at home we had made the national news. We were relieved that the day had passed peacefully, and we were pleased that we had got the job done.

Over the next seven days we completed a lot of tasking to move troops and supplies up country. We carried out 24 hour 'on call' standby duties, we met the Russians at Pristina airport, and ferried diplomats to meetings with various political stakeholders. During these seven days the squadron crews worked tirelessly to get the job done. We had strict rules regarding crew duty, such as the amount of time we could fly in any 24-hour period. However, in order to get all of the tasking done we sometimes had to break these rules – perhaps extending our flying by 30 minutes or an hour. We did not do this lightly. We were blessed with fine flying conditions for the duration. We would always be intentional and consensual as a crew, openly discussing the situations and agreeing our limits. This heightened our awareness to keep an eye on each other for fatigue and any missed procedures. All this was due to a common recognition of the importance of the work we were doing. I learnt at that time that rules were important and sometimes it was also important to work beyond them.

After seven days the roads were open and the need to move troops and supplies by air had diminished. The tasking dried up and the crews were grounded. As a result, our fantastic engineers had some respite in which they could service the aircraft. To keep the aircraft flying during the operation many of the air frames were carrying snags – minor maintenance issues that would need some time to fix but did not need to stop the aircraft flying. After the seventh day of tasking, when the aircraft were grounded, only one remained serviceable out of seven, quite unusual and a reflection of how hard we had made the airframes work.

During the detachment to Kosovo I had learnt that Sarah was expecting again and everything in me wanted to be with her. However, we had a job to do in that country which had political and geographical significance. We had faced the potential of coming up against a potent and capable enemy. I'd had to be clear on what my values were and what the purpose of the job was. It required more than an intellectual reconciling. It required me to engage with my own heart and my own courage, choosing to go beyond my own comfort zone and on occasion breach operational limitations. By July our job was done, and I was ready to go home and support Sarah with her maternity.

* * *

Courage is easily my second favourite leadership quality after humility. Encouraging people is not simply a soft and gentle pat on the back for a job well done but the significant and life enhancing imparting of courage – equipping people to engage with their own inner courage by connecting with their beliefs, values and passions. For me, to encourage someone is to help them engage with their heart, their passion, and what is truly important to them. What gets you out of bed in the morning? Is it the need to pay the mortgage, take the children to school, join the rat-race on the daily commute? To be honest this is what tends to keep me *in* bed in the morning. Or is it to pursue a vision and a goal where we can make a contribution, and which will make a difference in the world?

When we can identify what inspires us and what is important to us we can experience a shift up in terms of drive and commitment. So much progress is not made because of fear; the fear that it may not work, the fear of the fear that it may not work, the fear of failure, the fear of uncertainty. Courage is the antithesis of fear and Marianne Williamson challenges us in our fears with her poem from 'A Return to Love':

"Our deepest fear is not that we are inadequate.
Our deepest fear is that we are powerful beyond measure.
It is our light, not our darkness, that most frightens us.
We ask ourselves, who am I to be brilliant, gorgeous,
handsome, talented and fabulous?
Actually, who are you not to be?
You are a child of God
Your playing small does not serve the world.
There is nothing enlightened about shrinking so that other
people won't feel insecure around you.
We are all meant to shine, as children do.
We were born to make manifest the glory of

God that is within us.
It is not just in some; it is in everyone.
And, as we let our own light shine, we unconsciously give other
people permission to do the same.
As we are liberated from our fear, our presence
automatically liberates others."
—Marianne Williamson

The way to overcome fear is to identify it, to name it and to choose to have the courage to believe that the job can be done. That means engaging with your heart and acknowledging the emotions that reside there. If you doubt this, then consider how it is your heart that soars when you are in love, or it seems to swell when you have a feeling of intense pride; equally how your heart sinks when you hear some devastating news. A close friend of mine has experienced a Takotsubo Cardiomyopathy, also known as 'heart shock' or broken heart syndrome. It is a condition with similar symptoms to a heart attack. It damages the heart. In my friends' case it was brought about by acute stress, anxiety, anger and fear – all emotions.

Courage is an emotion. We can choose to be in control of our emotions or we can let them control us. The opportunity here is that by being emotionally intelligent we can choose our emotions. We can therefore choose to be courageous and we can choose to be a leader. Courage is not the absence of fear; it is acting in spite of fear. You become more courageous when you choose to confront your fear, your pain, the perceived danger, the uncertainty or the intimidation. I don't say any of this lightly. Hearts can be strong, and hearts can be weak. Hearts can fail. But without the heart there can be no courage. We each have a heart and we have a choice to tune into what our heart tells us, and in doing so we can be courageous.

In Kosovo there was fear - fear of the unknown and fear of the perceived threats. However, in our hearts we *believed* we were doing the right thing. This was based on commitment to duty which in itself was a reflection of our values. Being in the military means that a lot of the purpose, identity, beliefs and values are taken for granted; I doubt someone would be in the military if these weren't aligned. Our values act as anchors for courage. However, in the corporate world I have found there is often a lack of purpose, there is misalignment around identity and confusion around beliefs and values. Does this matter? Where this is the case, I think it is a waste of resource and potential. Organisations and teams that thrive have a clarity of purpose and a clarity of intent. They are clear about their beliefs and values, so much so that they explicitly live them and hold each other to account over them. To challenge each other and hold each other to account takes courage, because it is risky, and the outcome may be uncertain. But it is the right thing to do.

Leaders are people who understand the purpose of their organisation exquisitely, and they are able to articulate it in simple, common language. Leaders engage with, role model and promote a distinct identity which lives out their values. And leaders do these things from the heart – not from a cerebral, rational stand point but from an emotionally intelligent and engaging position. When these leaders are faced with adversity and fear they know they can engage with their heart and from it they can draw upon their courage.

Questions for you from your navigator:

- What is your deepest fear?
- When were you at your happiest and most fulfilled?
- What would it take for you to be courageous?
- Who needs encouragement from you as a leader?

DETERMINATION

"I do not think that there is any other quality so essential to success of any kind as the quality of perseverance. It overcomes almost everything, even nature.
—John D. Rockefeller

"I have nothing to offer but blood, toil, tears, and sweat."
—Winston Churchill

"Failure cannot cope with persistence."
—Napoleon Hill

"I get knocked down, but I get up again."
—Chumbawamba

I think that anybody who has been in the military has at some point had to demonstrate some degree of determination. It was one of the nine personal leadership qualities that we assessed officer cadets for during my time as a Flight Commander at Initial Officer Training (IOT) at Royal Air Force College Cranwell from 2002 to 2005. When someone wants to join the military - whether it is out of a sense of patriotic duty or whether it is simply to play with the hardware - there are a series of selection processes and training courses to pass. The initial desire to join the military is the start of a long process which includes a conversation with a recruitment officer, a screening interview, a selection centre with aptitude tests, medical tests and assessment exercises. This is only the precursor to years of specialist training courses. In the case of specialist roles, such as aircrew, the screening and selection testing can be particularly stringent. And before any of this can begin there is the need for sound academic foundations along with a demonstration of achievements in many extra-curricular activities such as participation in team sports and supporting community activities.

My own journey into the RAF and becoming a navigator began when I was a teenager and I had a fascination with helicopters. Many Saturday afternoons would be spent watching the TV series 'Airwolf' and films such as 'Blue Thunder'. I hold to this day that the best films have a helicopter in them somewhere. I was intrigued by these machines that could overcome gravity and manoeuvre in such a dynamic fashion. I was in awe of the heroic stature of the big yellow Royal Air Force Search & Rescue helicopters, often seen flying during holidays to the coast or to the mountains. As a young teenager my mum paid for me to have a ride in a Jet Ranger helicopter along Southport beach…and I was hooked. Feeling the downdraft when rushing into the aircraft under the spinning rotor blades, hearing the engine power increase, and watching the ground through the Perspex screen skim beneath my feet – it was fantastic. If I could do anything *close* to flying a helicopter in the future, I would take it.

So, at the age of 16 – and the year that the movie 'Top Gun' was screening in cinemas - I went to the local Armed Forces Career Office (AFCO) in Stoke-on-Trent and began my own journey of determination. I was advised that I could apply for a flying scholarship. This was funding from the Royal Air Force for me to learn how to fly a small aeroplane and gain a Private Pilot's Licence whilst attending Sixth Form College. This sounded good to me, so I applied. I passed the preliminary requirements at the AFCO and I was invited to the Officers and Aircrew Selection Centre (OASC) which was then located at Royal Air Force Biggin Hill in Kent, for a four-day selection course. The first two days were a series of medical and aptitude tests that assessed my suitability and aptitude for being aircrew – either pilot or navigator – along with fighter controller and air traffic controller roles. Each of these roles required a demonstration of potential in specific skills, an aptitude test and a high IQ. There were also a series of medical examinations to pass such as hearing, eyesight, cardiovascular and so on. The second two days were focussed on assessing my potential to be a commissioned officer in the Royal Air Force and involved a series of leadership assessments. These included an in-depth interview with two Boarding Officers, a group discussion, a group exercise, an individual problem to solve with a presentation, an individual command task where I would lead a team and a team command task where all candidates were equals. At the end of the four days I was invited to a debrief with two of the Boarding Officers. My aptitude scores to be a pilot in the Royal Air Force were not good enough and they would not be offering me a flying scholarship. I was thanked for my attendance and made my way home. I was disappointed.

I learnt some time later that attending OASC was not a one-off event and that I could apply again. After all, many changes take place through adolescence so maybe my aptitude for being a pilot had improved? So, in the first year of my undergraduate studies I applied again – this time for a Cadetship. A Cadetship meant sponsorship through University with a guaranteed place at IOT afterwards. I passed the local careers office tests and interviews and I was again invited to OASC at Royal Air Force Biggin Hill. This time I knew what to expect but it was still nerve-wracking. As before, on the final day I was invited into the room with the two Boarding Officers for a debrief. Once again, my aptitude scores to be a pilot were not good enough and as they were only awarding Cadetships to pilots as far as I was aware then my application was unsuccessful. I was even more disappointed. In fact, I was devastated…since I'd learnt that candidates were only allowed to undertake the pilot aptitude test twice. So, my chances of being a pilot in the Royal Air Force, or any of the UK armed forces for that matter - since they all used the OASC facility for pilot aptitude testing - were apparently zero.

I continued with my undergraduate studies and I was still being drawn to a career in the military – the selection processes I had been through had made me aware of the lifestyle and access to adventure that a life in the military could offer. I explored my options one more time. It had been a couple of years since my Cadetship application; I had worked hard to bolster my resume - I was now a Queen's Scout, a proficient kayak instructor and I played basketball and rugby for my University. In addition, I was an active member on a number of student committees. I learnt that I could apply for a bursary – funding for my remaining terms at University – and if successful I would be expected to join a University Air Squadron and then be offered a place at IOT after graduation. The bursary was not limited to aircrew; any officer branch would be considered for sponsorship. After a bit more research, I fancied applying to be a Royal Air Force Regiment Officer – effectively the Royal Air Force's own 'soldiers' who protected Royal Air Force stations in the UK and overseas. It was a role that promised adventure and leadership. In my mind I decided that I would apply for this Cadetship and if I was unsuccessful then I would try one more time after I'd graduated from University as a graduate entrant. That would be four attempts, and if I remained unsuccessful, I would get the message.

I applied for the bursary and again was invited to OASC, but this time only for the latter two days of selection. I did not need to attend the first two days again as all of the tests results for pilot, navigator, fighter controller and air traffic controller were on file and some could not be repeated anyway – besides, I was applying for a ground branch. Instead, I was invited to the second two days focussing on the officer selection part of the process. I felt well prepared this time, knowing what was coming and having acted on feedback from previous debriefs regarding confidence and assertiveness. At the end of the two days came the debrief with the Boarding Officers.

"Mr Cartlidge" they started, "…we note that you have applied to be a Regiment Officer?"

"That's right Sir." I replied, and there was some explanation from me on what I hoped to achieve from that role.

"Well, looking at your results from previous visits to OASC we note that you are in fine health and passed all of the aptitude tests very well, with the exception of the pilot motor skills. In fact, your navigator test scores improved on your second visit."

This was news to me and somewhat reassuring.

"On that basis we would like you to consider our offer to award you a bursary for the General Duties/Navigator branch."

Wow. I could be aircrew after all – even if it would ultimately be in the back seat of a jet. I accepted. My determination had paid off. And when I eventually graduated with my degree, I was one of only two people from my University course who had a job waiting for them.

That was the start of the journey. The need for determination and persistence did not stop there. Following my degree studies at

University I attended Royal Air Force College Cranwell for a 24-week Initial Officer Training Course. The 24 weeks were divided in to three phases and after each phase there would be a review when a number of cadets would be back-coursed to resit a phase or be 'chopped', meaning their Royal Air Force career was over. I passed IOT first time and learnt at the end of the course that I'd finished in the top twenty percent of my intake. Following this came a nine-month Basic Navigation Course (BNC), learning navigation techniques on the Bulldog, Tucano and Dominie aircraft at Royal Air Force Finningley near Doncaster, South Yorkshire. I was the only student who started my course to complete it first time; the others were either back-coursed or chopped. After the BNC came 'streaming' – the decision on whether I would go fast jet, multi-engine or rotary wing (helicopters). There was an informal ceremony in the Officer's Mess bar to announce the decision. My course tutor presented me with a baseball cap with an axe in it. Shit. Had I actually been chopped? My heart sank, and I began to feel embarrassed in front of the crowd in the bar. But then my instructor, somewhat relishing the confusion on my face, pointed out "it's a 'chopper' Rich. I was elated - I was going to be sent rotary wing. Historically the Royal Air Force had only sent pilots to rotary wing. However, in the mid 1990s, due to a shortage of pilots, navigators could also be sent rotary to sit alongside pilots and operate the aircraft. My boyhood dream to fly helicopters was getting closer.

After a short holding period following my BNC, I was posted to Royal Air Force Shawbury in Shropshire and I started a twelve-month Advanced Flying Training (AFT) course, initially flying the single engine Gazelle helicopter followed by the multi engine Wessex helicopter. At the end of this course students were awarded their flying badges - pilots were awarded their wings and navigators were awarded their brevets. I also was awarded the Group Captain Harding Trophy for best navigator student on the course. The only remaining decision now was which helicopter type I would be sent to fly. This was determined by the need of the service and the aptitude required to operate the aircraft, with small consideration given to my preferences. At the time there was much rivalry between which was the best helicopter to fly with. Wessex and Puma were the workhorses in Northern Ireland, where the Troubles were still high profile. However, I was attracted to the Chinook HC Mk 2 helicopter, arguably the most capable helicopter in the British Military both then and now – and I got my wish.

I was posted to the Operational Conversion Unit (OCU) for the Chinook HC Mk 2 Helicopter at Royal Air Force Odiham, Hampshire. This was a six-month flying course that familiarised me with the specifics of the helicopter type and prepared me for operational duty. I was the only ab-initio[8] on the OCU. All of my course mates were pilots, navigators and crewmen who were transferring from other aircraft types. I passed first time, joined No. 7 Squadron and worked towards becoming combat ready...the final step to mark the end of my journey to be an operational navigator on front line service in the Royal Air Force. Within 6 months of joining the Squadron I was combat ready, and I had two medals to show for it - both campaign medals for service in Northern Ireland and Bosnia.

At the age of 26 I had achieved my boyhood dream from more than ten years previously – to fly in helicopters. In the following years of operational service, I was given the opportunity to actually pilot the Chinook helicopter on three different continents in a variety of

---

[8] Ab-initio – a student aircrew who is passing through the training system for the first time.

conditions. Many pilots would be keen to know that their left-hand seat operator, meaning their navigator – me, could adequately handle and land the aircraft in the event of injury or emergency. So, I got to fly and operate one of the longest serving, most capable, formidable and recognisable aircraft that is still in service in the Royal Air Force today.

* * *

As a navigator in the Royal Air Force much of my working life was dominated by latitude and longitude. That simple code of a dozen or so digits would locate me anywhere in the world within metres – in the northern hemisphere, the southern hemisphere and any of the four continents that I had the opportunity to fly over. Latitude and longitude tell us where we are in the world. Their co-ordinates can be used to define the destination we need to get to. Maps and charts are distinguished by the framework of grid lines laid upon them to illustrate where a particular piece of geography fits in the world.

Most of us, most of the time do not need to think about latitude and longitude or of the precision needed for navigation. We follow well defined routes habitually to work, to school, to the sports club etc. Often these routes are prescribed to us through our smart phone or sat nav system. When we stray from our routine, perhaps on holiday, we are channelled along routes to the airport, to the plane, to the connection, to the hotel. Automated navigation that accurately tells us where to go has become a taken-for-granted mainstay of our modern way of living. Even when we need to go somewhere new, unfamiliar or different it is rare that we may have to do some actual plotting. We merely need to put the name of our destination into a device and we will be given route options to choose from and follow.

Of course, it wasn't always so. I want to acquaint you with one of my heroes who came 39th in the BBC's 2002 public poll of the 100 Greatest Britons; someone who showed great determination in pursuit of a cause and who made a significant contribution to the lives of navigators – John Harrison.

In the 18th Century, advances in technology and exploration meant that the world was opening up to international trade – and the race was on to achieve global superiority to control the wealth and power that international trade afforded. But there was a problem. There was no accurate, established method for calculating longitude at sea. Once ships were out of sight of land they quickly became lost – at the expense of life and material. One of the greatest scientific challenges of the 18th century was the need for a reliable and accurate method for calculating longitude at sea. To solve this problem would result in huge commercial and strategic advantage for the country whose navy could accurately navigate, and subsequently command the oceans. The importance of finding a method to calculate longitude accurately led to the British government establishing the Longitude Act in July 1714:

"An Act for Providing a Publick Reward for such Person or Persons as shall Discover the Longitude at Sea' in July 1714."

The authors of the Act cited the importance of finding the longitude for the:

"Safety and Quickness of Voyages, the Preservation of Ships and the Lives of Men', the 'Trade of Great Britain' and 'the Honour of [the] Kingdom'."[9]

---

[9] Alexi Baker, History and Philosophy of Science. University of Cambridge https://cudl.lib.cam.ac.uk/view/ES-LON-00023

The prize was £20,000 – equivalent to millions of pounds in today's money. Most people, including the establishment, believed that astronomy would provide the answer to the longitude problem; but John Harrison, a Yorkshire born working-class carpenter from Lincolnshire, with an interest in horology, thought different.

At this point I want to highlight how latitude and longitude are derived. Latitude, the horizontal lines around the globe, is relatively easy to calculate. It can be done by measuring the inclination of the sun from the horizon at midday and consulting an almanac that will provide the seasonal data to calculate latitude. However, longitude – the vertical lines around the globe - requires an accurate method for measuring between reference points. If you consider the world, like a circle, is divided into 360°, and the world rotates once every 24 hours, then each degree of longitude is four minutes of time. 15° of longitude is one hour. So, if you know the time at a reference point, say Greenwich in the United Kingdom, and you know when it is midday at your location then you can calculate your longitude. For example, if it is midday at your location (because the sun is at its highest point in the sky for the day) and you somehow also know that at that moment in Greenwich it is 3pm, then you can deduce that you are 45° west of Greenwich.

John Harrison recognised this method and he embarked on what would become a lifelong quest to design and build a timepiece that would accurately keep time on board ships. This was no straightforward feat since the mechanical solution would need to accurately operate withstanding various conditions such as ferocious storms, the constant movement of the ship at sea, and the corrosive properties of salty sea air. Only then would he be worthy of the longitude prize. Achieving this task took him decades and at one point the Board of Longitude, the body of experts set up to administer the prize, only awarded him half of the monies. Nevertheless, with his fourth timepiece called H4, John Harrison produced a game changing piece of technology. H4 was sufficiently reliable to provide a proven way to navigate accurately at sea. The competitive advantage realised meant that in due course the Royal Navy could take the opportunity to achieve global supremacy. For the next two centuries Britain ruled the waves and a large contribution to this in my view was because a working-class carpenter laboured with determination for over forty years to see his vision and dream completed.

The story of John Harrison and the Longitude Prize – more fully described in Dava Sobel's book 'Longitude' – is another example of why determination is my third favourite leadership quality. Any significant endeavour that I can think of, any significant achievement in sport, business, science, personal health, art or any other discipline requires determination, usually coupled with a lot of hard work. It is almost inevitable that part of the journey will encounter adversity of some sort – John Harrison faced criticism and rejection – and yet I am convinced that adversity forges leadership. When adversity comes leaders are the ones who through their determination and persistence can hold onto a vision and continue against the odds until the task is done. Along the way they are presented with the choice of whether to continue or not - is it worth it? If it is worth it, then the leader must be determined to carry on until the destination is reached – *per ardua ad astra.*

The famous quote at the start of this chapter by Winston Churchill is an example to me of someone who had the odds against them and no surety of success and yet was convinced, and had the belief in himself, and the cause, that the work would continue until the task was complete. For John Harrison this meant constructing a timepiece that would win the longitude prize. In my own modest experience of pursuing a career in the Royal Air Force to fly helicopters it meant trying several times and working hard through many years of training courses to realise the goal.

What does it mean in your situation right now?

In all of these examples the individuals set themselves on a course towards a clear goal. To work on their goal, they had to make best use of the time they had. I am intrigued by the role that time plays in leadership. When things aren't going the way we'd like them to time can seem to pass slowly. Paradoxically, when things go wrong in highly dynamic situations they can go wrong very quickly, and time seems to accelerate. Within these situations I believe determination is the attitudinal choice that we make to continue to pursue the goal. As we know from the longitude story, time can be used to inform us of where we are; knowledge of time is needed to help us to accurately navigate to where we want to get to. Journeys take time. For me, determination is the quality that means that we choose to push through to the goal as time passes, whatever the circumstances may be telling us. Without determination we can drift and lose hope. Determination engages with the beliefs and desires of the heart, the courageous aspirations that leaders can envision, and it is uncompromising in reaching its destination. As leaders we need to be wise to the many things that can derail our determination to get something done. I offer three for consideration here, maybe you can identify more:

- Is the mission important enough?
- Discouragement.
- It's easy not to…

Is the mission important enough? Often in coaching conversations, if there is a lack of progress then the questioning will turn to 'commitment' - how much does the client *really* want to achieve the goal. Most of us want to do many things, and there are many gurus out there who will say that anything is possible. A friend of mine says that as long as you have your health then anything is achievable. I suppose the point is that this is only the case if you want to achieve it enough. Do you have a goal or a mission that is so compelling that it will fuel a determination of spirit that pushes through any adversity and setback and sacrifice? During the dark hours, the hard yards, the lowest ebbs and amongst the nay-sayers do you actually believe that you can reach the destination?

Discouragement. It isn't necessarily inevitable that there will be setbacks – but in any worthy cause I'd say they are likely. Dealing with setbacks, failure and rejection requires a choice on whether to give up or whether to choose to be determined and press on.

Part of my BNC aircrew training at Royal Air Force Finningley required passing a survival course, one of several that had to be completed at various stages of training. During a classroom session ahead of the practical component of the course a young Flight Sergeant was practising some amateur psychology. On the whiteboard was a quadrant with two axes: one of introvert versus extrovert and the other axis I honestly cannot remember. However, the Flight Sergeant asked us to close our eyes and raise our hand if we were in the lower right quadrant. I remember this was something to do with being an introvert and so I raised my hand.

"Open your eyes." he instructed the group. I was the only one with my hand raised.

He looked me in the eye, pointed at me, and said:

"You will not pass aircrew training."

My course colleagues looked a little bemused and I was not a little surprised by the severity of his tone. Apparently, I did not have the right personality, according to his quadrant exercise, to be aircrew in the Royal Air Force. It would have been easy to be discouraged at this point and potentially to give up, especially as I was the only one in the room to have raised my hand to be publicly belittled. However, I wasn't going to give up on the basis of this exercise. Determination to work towards what we believe in and what we want can be a powerful thing and, eventually, I was the only person in that room to pass that particular BNC.

It's easy not to... During my tour at Royal Air Force College Cranwell there was a period where a colleague, Matt, and I worked together closely in an office. We both had sons of similar ages. We often remarked in the late winter months that it would be good to take the boys camping and have a 'lads and dads' weekend later in the year. We both enjoyed the outdoors, so what could be more wholesome than a weekend away in a National Park somewhere enjoying the outdoors and quality time in friendship and with our boys? Well, spring came and went; summer came and went and before we knew it, we were in the office on a grey, cold November day reflecting that we had not taken the boys camping and climbing and walking and kayaking. Perhaps an opportunity had been missed. How did this happen? We concluded it was *'easy not to'* – any time we had come close to the opportunity to go on a mini-adventure there was always a pitiful excuse not to – for example a domestic commitment, a less than perfect weather forecast, some equipment we thought we needed but didn't have. All of these obstacles were surmountable…but it was *easy not to*. It is often easier to be lazy, not bother and lack commitment. There are always excuses not to do the things that we know would bring us joy and fulfilment in the long run. I have since had some amazing trips with my son (& daughter) to National Parks, concerts, sporting fixtures, holidays and more. Every time it would have been easier not to – but I know my life would be a little less rich as a result.

Questions from your navigator:

- Where are you saying "it's easy not to" right now?
- Where does your encouragement come from?
- How compellingly important is your goal?
- What is your level of commitment to achieving it?
- How will you get in your own way?
- How determined are you to see it through?

LEADERSHIP PRINCIPLES

CAPACITY

The working day started at 0800 with a met brief[10]. There was always an element of childlike anticipation to find out which areas of the country would be favourable for flying that day. I always had my fingers crossed that the weather in the north west would be most suitable…that meant that the Lake District would be 'open' to fly through. I would spend most of my Sunday afternoons in late summer and early autumn in flight planning, creating routes that I would visualise flying in the coming weeks. Flight planning was in a room adjacent to one of the hangars at Royal Air Force Finningley, Doncaster. During the working week there would be the constant sound (and smell) of piston engine and turbo-prop aircraft starting up, taxi-ing, taking off and flying from and to the airfield. However, on a Sunday afternoon there was silence – except for the gentle metal rattling of the secured hangar doors in the wind. It was 1993 and I was a student navigator on No. 425 Basic Navigation Course at No. 6 Flight Training School; and I was on the 'Tucano' phase of training.

The Short Tucano is a two-seat turboprop basic trainer used by the Royal Air Force to train pilots and navigators during the basic phases of their respective courses. I had not given much consideration to what the role of a navigator was – other than for my own circumstances that it was a route to becoming aircrew in an air force steeped in history, and an opportunity to fly in some serious hardware. At this stage of my career I did not know whether I would be a navigator on helicopters, multi-engine aircraft or the back seat of

---

[10] Meteorological Brief – a daily briefing on the weather forecast for the day.

a Panavia Tornado fast jet – but I was loving the planning and organising that was required to complete a flying sortie along with learning all of the new techniques required to successfully achieve missions. Little did I realise at this stage, that the skills I was mastering as a navigator – to successfully get from A to B through a myriad of conditions – would evolve in my career beyond the Royal Air Force and serve me with an identity and a practice to nurture and develop leaders in the future.

Royal Air Force Finningley, Doncaster

On the Tucano Phase student navigators had to pass 22 sorties covering various navigation techniques and emergency procedures as well as developing airmanship. All of the training was focussed on what would come next, meaning that if we were successful – there was a significant failure rate - we would progress to more sophisticated aircraft. This was part of a three-year journey from joining the Royal Air Force to arriving on a front-line Squadron ready for operational duties. Throughout aircrew training we were exposed to increasing amounts of complexity and more systems to manage and understand. The training varied from aviation medicine and understanding the effects of hypoxia (oxygen starvation at altitude) - essential to allow us to wear the integrated AEA[11] and survival equipment when we strapped ourselves to an ejector seat - through to raw navigation practices of understanding navigation beacons, managing multiple radios and being proficient at mental dead reckoning (MDR) – the skill of computing speed, time and drift calculations quickly and accurately in the airborne environment. The technical training was also interspersed with survival training and

---

[11] Aircrew Equipment Assembly – various pieces of equipment to allow aircrew to function in the cockpit e.g. oxygen mask, 'g'- pants, helmet etc.

leadership development.

The term that came up consistently and was always assessed on any sortie was 'airmanship'. It was never really clear to me back then what this term precisely meant. I knew it had something to do with having a generally sound and holistic sense of what was going on at any time whilst airborne. Good airmanship meant that I knew what was going on in myself, in the cockpit, in the aircraft and in the 'bigger picture' around me - and thus I could anticipate what was going to happen next. I could make sense of the situation. Poor airmanship meant that I was 'behind' the aircraft, reacting to circumstances and certainly in no position to control outcomes – a dangerous state to be in and one where it was a struggle to make sense of a situation. In these situations I would be prone to behaving in a reactive way rather than a proactive way. Distraction and anxiety, mental or physical – the airborne environment in a military aircraft can be physiologically stressful - would narrow my attention span and cause me to focus on the wrong thing at that time. I realised it was in these instances that what I was deficient in, what I was lacking – was capacity.

When the weather was suitable north west it meant I could go flying low level through the Lake District…easily one of my top five places in the world due to the memories, personal experiences and sheer beauty of the place. As a teenager I had enjoyed many visits to The Lake District: either character forming adventures with my Venture Scout Unit or many fell-walking weekends with my Dad. Even then I used to love pouring over maps and designing routes which would then be walked and explored. I used to love seeing what the terrain actually looked like 'for real', navigating in different conditions of snow or low cloud or glorious sunshine, and I enjoyed the sense of accomplishment when a peak had been successfully scaled. And now

I had the privilege to view many of those memorable places from a bird's eye perspective; albeit travelling a tad faster than a bird.

As a student navigator, when it came time to do a training flight the sortie number would go up on the operations room's daily programme board. The instructor and I would brief the sortie. This involved 'walking' through the route, highlighting any hazards or notifications to be aware of and discussing the objectives of the sortie. There would be some testing of understanding such as what would happen during various emergency situations – and then we would be good to go. We walked to the safety equipment section to collect our flying kit – life jackets, flying helmets, survival vests etc. The instructor would brief the duty authorising officer and sign orders for the sortie followed by signing for the aircraft from the engineers which would include any last-minute updates to our aircraft's serviceability. In the meantime, I would have walked to the aircraft, carried out some checks and strapped in. With the instructor strapped in and the canopy closed the aircraft would be started and we were in our own sanitised world for the next two hours. To get to this stage was such a privilege – to be in a Royal Air Force aircraft and to go flying. Of course, there was always pressure to perform and pass the sortie, but it was also a thrill. We would taxi to the runway, get clearance for take-off, countdown to start our stopwatches together and then the pilot released the brakes. The Tucano accelerated down the runway and we launched into the air. I'm not sure any aviator gets tired of take-offs and landings – the surge of power, increasing speed, the rattling of the machine and the whooshing of air as the speed builds. Meanwhile the pilot instructor and I would have in our helmets the crisp, clipped radio transmissions that connected us beyond the airframe to air traffic control - some of the wider team involved to make all of this work.

We would be one of scores of training sorties operating from the base that day.

Heading out of Royal Air Force Finningley's airspace we travelled north past Castleford and Harrogate, turning west and deliberately routing to the south of Malham Cove, mostly for the view – why wouldn't you? We skirted the Yorkshire Dales and flew to the south end of Windermere.

Plotting a route and then flying it is where the first principle of making capacity came alive for me. The route would be divided into legs and each leg would be carefully marked out on a chart with headings and timings. Timing is everything in navigation – and the importance of time to you as a leader is a theme that features elsewhere in this book. As with most things in the military there is a drill and a checklist. To fly along a leg of the route, I would brief the pilot on Heading, Airspeed and Time (HAT) meaning what heading was he to fly, at what speed and for how long. From take-off to landing, every leg of the journey had a HAT to follow. Correspondingly, there was a sequencing brief that organised the process. Approaching a turning point – which would be confirmed visually and hopefully by accurate timing – I would brief the pilot on the HAT required on the next leg. Flying over the turning point I would restart the stopwatch, the pilot would turn onto the new heading, adjusted for drift using MDR, and I would confirm the new HAT were accurate. I would then confirm the next event, namely the next turning point or initials point that would be in, for example, three minutes and forty-five seconds. At 210kts airspeed we would cover just over 13 nautical miles in three minutes and forty-five seconds. I then knew that I had those three minutes and forty-five seconds to do other things – this was CAPACITY. Primarily at this stage of training this meant lookout...lookout of the cockpit for things that might kill us, such as the ground, wires, bird strikes or other aircraft. At this stage of relatively basic flying training this was an important habit to consolidate and would develop that all important airmanship. As I progressed onto more sophisticated aircraft and more complex missions this capacity would be used up by competing demands such as complex communications, more sophisticated aircraft systems to manage, crew management, stress and other pressures. But for now, I was consolidating the habit of *making capacity* through the next event technique – a skill that would serve me well in the future as a mission commander. Flying north along Windermere, over the Kirkstone Pass and down into the Ullswater valley, my capacity gave me the freedom to enjoy the view and reminisce with gratitude the many adventures I had experienced in that marvellous place with others years earlier. When I got home at night, I would phone home and relay to Dad the sortie details of the route flown, and the familiar places seen, and I would think *'even if they 'chop'[12] me tomorrow, they can't take that memory away.'*

* * *

In the corporate world of today there seems to be a 'busy busy' epidemic or perhaps a 'busy' virus. The common daily greeting appears to be something like this; Susan: "Hi Bob, how are you?" Bob: "Fine thanks, really busy...you?" Susan: "Yes, good. Busy."

What is all this busyness about? There seems to be an ironic comfort in people feeling busy and conveying this to colleagues. I wonder if this has something to do with self-worth; or maybe it's connected to a sub-conscious need to avoid being seen to have spare time.

---

[12] 'chop' – to be removed from the course due to poor progress

Calendars and diaries are filled with back to back meetings as if some weird version of Tetris was being played and punishing schedules prohibit any spare time to think or have any capacity. I am curious as to whether having come through years of recession and austerity with corresponding 're-structures', the corporate populous is not a little paranoid that if you're not 'busy' then you don't have enough to do, and your job can be, well, restructured. Alternatively, being busy may be perceived as being successful – when actually the opposite would make more sense.

Take a five-day working week…notionally 37.5 hours contracted in a full-time job. I believe that managers fill those 37.5 hours with meetings and activities and 'stuff' and at the end of the week they will say "I got my week done but I'm *really* busy." And of course, it probably took more than five days or 37.5 hours to complete. Often it includes late night working and in particular Sunday evening emailing 'just to get ahead of Monday morning' - compromising time with family and loved ones. Please don't misunderstand me here, I think management is really important – you have to be able to manage to lead. But here's my challenge: I believe leaders do all of the things managers do in three days and they spend the other two days doing what leaders do – building relationships, reflecting, contingency planning, exploring perspectives, thinking differently etc. Normally this statement gets the reaction - at least in people's heads - *"don't you know how busy I am – that's fantasy?"* Well, here's the rub…people who get promoted don't get given an extra day in the week. Somehow, they work out how to make capacity and prioritise, honour the mission, think differently, delegate and empower others so that they can focus on what's most important. This is the antidote to the busy virus which is epidemic in some corporate settings and is having a negative effect on well-being and resilience. How resilient we are is often seen as a reactive response to events. If we can make capacity, we can be proactive and build up our resilience to events and improved performance will follow. The antidote is leadership – it's not about abdication; rather, with humility, it's about thinking of others and empowering them, because people have the potential to be brilliant. People are often not given credit for how capable they can be. The leader's responsibility in this is to make sure that as the leader, they maintain if not create capacity, so that they can keep an eye on progress against the big picture, they have thinking space for contingency planning to cope with the unexpected, they can identify where people can be used best, they monitor the welfare of their people and they identify emerging obstacles that need removing. Because if the leader isn't doing this, then maybe no-one will.

In case you're thinking this is far-fetched then allow me to share an example. I led a leadership programme for high potential senior managers in a £1.2Bn organisation of twelve thousand people. One of the delegates, Nigel, responded cynically to my challenge of being 'busy' with the exasperated and incredulous response of *'don't you know how busy I am?'* Nigel was working up to 80 hours per week (he was contracted to do 37.5 hours); he was regularly home late - after his young daughter's bedtime - and he was not happy. Following my provocative and somewhat cantankerous challenge, and after participating in the leadership programme, Nigel learnt how to be a better leader, to prioritise and to make capacity! One year later Nigel fed back that he was regularly working closer to 40+ hours per week, he was home every night in time for bath-time with his two-year-old daughter, and then he would walk the dog for some quality 'me' time. This was without any detriment to Nigel's performance in his professional role and he actually moved to a more productive role shortly afterwards. As a result of the leadership programme I led,

Nigel moved from being a busy, work stressed manager to a resilient and productive leader with much better wellbeing. Nigel learnt the importance of making capacity for himself and thereby he had space to practice being a better leader.

Still not convinced?

I recently met a new friend who is in charge of the IT department in a large UK Police Force. Sam was participating in a leadership programme that I was running. At the start of Day 1 we did a check-in where there was the usual discussion around 'busy' virus. There was the characteristic agreement that everybody was too busy, and that life was hectic with no space to do 'the important stuff'. Sam disagreed. He ran a section where 10% of work time was dedicated to personal (IT related) projects - akin to practices in Google and 3M. His colleagues were aghast…how could he do this? "It isn't always easy," Sam explained "but we made a decision to go for it and we do it. It's a mind-set and an attitude." My heart leapt. I know that it is possible to 'make capacity'; after all, as I said earlier, when people are promoted they don't get given an extra day in their week – so to be a great leader we need to learn how to do this through prioritising, focussing and being disciplined with how we use our time. Some people say what gets measured gets done. I think what we choose to focus on and believe becomes reality. So, if we focus on being busy, we become busy. If we focus on making capacity, we make capacity. This usually involves some honesty and decisiveness about how we organise ourselves. Sam's example was encouraging. In the past 12 months he has had *two* people leave his section for considerably better paid jobs in the private sector…only to return within months to ask for their old job back…because of the culture that Sam had created, nurtured and maintained. They enjoyed having the capacity to work on their own 'stuff' as part of their job.

So, I want you to think about how you use your time. Of course, capacity is more than just having more time – it's about greater awareness and attention and focus – but it starts with creating more time in your schedule called life. We've all heard the adage 'time is money' – but this doesn't make sense to me. Money is something we can get more of, it is something we can lose, it is a variable. Time is a constant…I can guarantee you that you will have 24 hours tomorrow; and how you spend them is up to you. In fact, I can also guarantee you 365 days in a year, minimum; and how you spend them will be up to you. If you fill your time with the wrong stuff you will erode your capacity – and it is you who is doing this. In the Tucano cockpit I had to manage the time I had between waypoints with great discipline. I could not afford to do things that did not contribute to the mission. I was training to build capacity as a routine practice so that I was able to adapt the plan to achieve the mission as and when the inevitable and unexpected curve balls appeared.

In aviation time is fuel, or perhaps more accurately fuel is time…but 'time is fuel' sounds better to me. A full tank of aviation fuel on a Chinook helicopter would give me about two and a half hours of flying time to work with. I had to make sure that what I did in those two and a half hours achieved the mission. If I needed longer, I needed more fuel, so I had to plan for this. When airborne, it was imperative that fuel was monitored: failure to do so would end catastrophically, as has been the case on too many occasions. Anyone who has seen the 2017 film Dunkirk will recognise this as Tom Hardy's character ended up drifting his fuel starved Spitfire onto the beach and sacrificing himself to capture by the enemy. You'd think it could not be possible to run out of fuel in this day and age with smart monitoring, warning systems and high-level training for aircrew, but failure to pay attention to fuel still happens with unfortunate regularity; and it has tragic consequences. On 28th November 2016, LaMia Flight 2933, a charter flight carrying the Brazilian Chapecoense football squad and their entourage, crashed near Medellín, Colombia, killing 71 of the 77 people on board. The cause of the crash? All four engines shut down due to fuel starvation.

In life and business, it is the same. Time is fuel. Perceptibly there is never enough time, it is compressed, and it is managed really badly, with the consequence that everyone is 'busy'. I want to challenge this. In my experience great leaders make capacity, and what they do with this capacity defines them. My favourite thing that leaders do with their capacity is they think differently about their circumstances and then, if necessary, they change them. In fact, great leaders 'make time' for the important things, like relationships, networks, results, performance and so on. As I mentioned earlier, I can guarantee how much time you will have tomorrow and next year; and as a leader your mission is to make sure that you manage it exquisitely so that you don't run out of it, you don't crash, and you DO achieve the mission. In fact, I'd encourage you to be so brilliant at this that you always have a little left over for the end sortie – so that like the main character Maverick in the movie 'Top Gun', you can always request a fly by at the end …because it's fun.

We have to pay for fuel and that makes us think about how we use it. Time is fuel. Fuel is getting more expensive. Time is valuable. You get a finite amount. Is this simply an exercise in prioritization, or a change in mindset? Stop doing the unproductive things, certainly stop wasting time and start managing it in a way that gets your mission accomplished. Here's a quick exercise: imagine your diary for tomorrow, or your next working day, was wiped clean. What are the 3 things you would really want to do with that time? Now look at what you have got planned and see if they match. If not, what can you take responsibility for - without making excuses or blaming other people - to start making your time serve you? Could you empower others to contribute to your mission? When you take control of your schedule you will notice an increased capacity to focus on the important, mission critical things. This is a mindset issue; whether you believe you can create capacity or whether you believe you cannot create capacity, then you're probably right[13].

Questions from your navigator:

- Do you need more capacity?
- Who is in control of your diary?
- Where could you start to make time, prioritise, increase capacity?

---

[13] "Whether you think you can or whether you think you can't, you're right." Henry Ford.

THINKING DIFFERENTLY

"Insanity: doing the same things over and over again and expecting different results."
"If at first an idea is not absurd then there is no hope for it."
—Albert Einstein

We had been sat around the crew room all day wondering if any tasking would come in. Crew room sounds luxurious, but it was actually a plain room with some soft chairs located at one end of an aged aircraft hangar. Outside it wasn't very warm; it was a grey, winters day in January at Divulje Barracks near to the Croatian town of Split. The highlight of the day was visiting the rations store, an ISO[14] container full of chocolates and high energy foods that we could take flying with us. As a child the thought of unfettered access to the tuck shop would have been wildly exciting. But when you know the combination lock code and have free access the novelty of helping yourself to a schoolboy's tuck shop dream of treats was somewhat diminished. The crews who had been on tasks that day had all returned and were heading to the bar for their first beer of the evening. Our crew was on 24hr standby duty – so no beers. Outside, it was getting dark, the air was chilling, and the lights were coming on in the villages across the water in Arbanija and Slatine, the light reflecting and bouncing off the ripples

---

[14] What we called the ISO container should more accurately be described as an intermodal container – a large standardised metal shipping container designed and built for freight transport. ISO is 'International Organisation for Standardisation'; a standards setting body.

in the Adriatic Sea. With a layer of cloud cover there was no warm sunset to enjoy and there would be no stars to view.

The news came in. There had been a fire 'up country' in Bosnia at an old bus station in Mrkonjic Grad where 26th Armoured Engineer Squadron were based. Sleeping bags, camp beds, clothing and other kit had been destroyed in the fire and dozens of troops were now facing the prospect of a night in sub-zero temperatures. A C-130 Hercules transport aircraft had already been despatched from the UK loaded with emergency supplies. However, the closest it would be able to get to the bus station was Split airport – still over 100 miles away. It would arrive at Split in one hour. We had to get ready. We needed to brief the mission, plan the route, prepare the aircraft and get dressed for flying in sub-zero conditions. These were early days in the detachment and we were wary of the threats from the enemy, not to mention the threats from flying at night in winter conditions in an unfamiliar terrain. I was anxious but also excited. This was real and the sort of work I had spent the past three years training for.

The plan was that we would hop over to the airport in our CH47 Chinook ready to meet the C-130 aircraft. We did not have anything like the cargo capacity of the C-130 so we would prioritise the most important kit, such as warm clothes, bedding and heaters, and transfer it to the Chinook, loading it as efficiently as possible so that the troops would have what they needed to survive the next few nights. We would then head up country as quickly as possible to deliver the goods. We briefed, walked to the aircraft and got started on the mission. It was January 1996 and I was on my first operational detachment with No.7 Squadron. We were supporting IFOR in the Former Yugoslavian Republic. I had to work out a route plan for how we would get the supplies from sea level to 3000' above sea level, 120 miles into a potentially hostile country, at night, in sub-zero temperatures with thick cloud cover and with a forecast for poor weather. If we didn't achieve the mission our army colleagues would be in for an even harder night.

There was 8/8 of cloud cover up country – this meant a total blanket of cloud with no breaks – and there was snow in the air. We would need to be mindful of our icing limits to fly up to the landing site at low level staying below the cloud – there would be no other way to reach the troops. Using Night Vision Goggles (NVGs) we would follow a route I had planned to follow the valleys and key reference points as best we could. The maps we were using were not as detailed or familiar as the UK maps that I was used to from my navigator training. The accuracy of where hazards were plotted – such as wires and pylons – was uncertain. We had to be cautious. My first operational tour, flying in freezing conditions, at night, in a degrading weather situation in a country where there was still a threat of hostile enemy action towards us. Awesome. Fortunately, I was teamed up with an experienced Special Forces (SF) crew for whom this sort of thing was familiar and somewhat routine.

We started the Chinook engines and flew the few hundred yards across to the apron at Split Airport where the C-130 had just landed and parked. By now it was properly dark, and the area was bathed in an amber glow from the apron's floodlights. We taxied so that our cabin ramp was facing the C-130's ramp and the crewman and Royal Air Force personnel from the airport quickly got to work transferring kit between the aircraft. I programmed our navigation equipment with the route plan whilst our two crewmen Martin and Rick did an outstanding job of efficiently filling all the space in the cabin with boxes of supplies, there was no point ferrying fresh air to our customers. By the time they had finished loading they could not see each other across the cabin which was full floor to ceiling and wall to wall, and the only way we knew Martin was at the back of the aircraft was because he was on the intercom. We carried out our pre-flight checks and launched into the dark winter's night.

We made steady progress flying at low level and eventually reached the sports pitch which was to be our landing point, marked with a landing 'T' – a sequence of torches aligned into wind denoting a 'T' shape to mark our landing point - put out by JHSU[15] colleagues. There was a collection of troops ready to help with the unloading. It is a wonderful thing to be waiting for a Chinook on a cold night with precipitation in the air and only the sound of the wind for company. At first, you think you hear the characteristic low beating 'wokka' sound somewhere in the distance, but you can't be sure as the sound comes and goes on the wind. But then it becomes more consistent and you become certain. Then very soon there is the overwhelming energy of the Chinook landing next to you; the forceful downdraft that can knock you off your feet, the noise of the whining gearboxes right on top of you drowning out all other sounds so much that you can hardly hear people shouting who are right next to you; the distinctive exhaust fumes wafting across the landing site as all the while the air beats from the thunderous wokka rotor blades – the vibration you can feel through your chest. If you've been waiting for a lift or waiting for relief supplies, it is a most welcome feeling. The pilot, Jim, skilfully landed the helicopter and the crewmen Martin and Rick quickly despatched the cargo with the eager assistance of some grateful army engineers. We could not loiter, fuel was limited, and we had to get back to Divulje Barracks. There was no desire to shut

---

[15] JHSU – Joint Helicopter Support Unit

down and risk being unable to re-start the aircraft. We would be unnecessarily vulnerable to local interest and we would have to spend the cold night in the CH47 Hilton which rarely delivered a good night's rest. After a few minutes we were ready to leave. We launched into the night sky, returning Mrkonjic Grad and the 26th Armoured Engineer Squadron to the peace of a dark wintry night. The grateful soldiers now had several tonnes of supplies to distribute amongst themselves.

Since the weather was deteriorating at low level, we decided to punch through the cloud cover and transit back to Split Airport, using our instruments rather than visual cues to navigate. We had the fuel to do this safely and we were within limits with the weather forecast at Split. All we needed to do was safely climb through the cloud layer, establish our heading at a safe altitude, establish communications with Split Airport, follow the navigation beacon signal to the overhead and carry out an ILS[16] landing. We initiated the climb and eventually settled at about Flight Level 80 (around 8,000') which was safely above any high ground on the transit back. It was dark, the aircraft was performing well and there was light discussion among the crew about the task we had just completed. At night in the cockpit we could either fly with normal light or 'black' light; the latter used when flying with NVGs. Since we were above cloud and flying on instruments, we reset to normal lighting which was a bit more relaxing and made it slightly easier to read the instruments. All was going well until 'dink' – we lost the instrumentation.

There was no jolt or sound, but the navigation instruments simply weren't giving any readings. Jim was flying the aircraft smoothly and still had his artificial horizon to follow, the engine dials and primary

---

[16] ILS – Instrument Landing System

instruments were all fine; but we had lost our navigation aids – the main compass and navigational pointers were frozen. Jim and I looked at each other quizzically across the dark cockpit. "Ok, check the cards," said Jim. We always flew with Fight Reference Cards (FRCs) which had checklists and drills for all known malfunctions. We cycled through the emergencies that could have caused an electrical problem, but nothing rectified the instruments. "Hmm…this is unusual." Jim said. I was flying with one of the most experienced Chinook crews in the Royal Air Force at the time…and they were stumped. Without navigation aids we would be unable to fly to the beacon at Split nor follow an approach into the airport. This was not good.

What we did have working was the RNS 252 GPS navigation system and the E2C compass, which worked as a simple magnetic compass. It was awkward to read and follow in the dark cockpit due to its location on top of the instrument coaming – but it was a reliable enough back up and accurate enough to keep us heading in the right direction. The RNS 252 was known to drift in position and required regular updating from external references every 20 minutes or so. It was a super piece of equipment for navigation, but it was not cleared for use as an internal aid for letdown procedures as its accuracy could not be guaranteed for the strict let down limits. So, we had to think of another way to get below 8/8 cloud cover and return to Split and Divulje Barracks before the fuel ran out.

In any operational tasking it was imperative to be in communications with AWACS, an E-3 sentry aircraft that would be on station 24/7 to monitor and co-ordinate aircraft movements in the theatre of operations. We had already been speaking to them with procedural, routine calls as part of the mission, and it was comforting to know we weren't alone, especially when they had a British accent. Jim had an idea. We would ask the AWACS to give us radar vectors to an area over the Adriatic clear of all terrain. We would use the RNS 252 to carry out an internal aid let down over the sea to get us below cloud. Once we were visual with the sea surface we would fly back towards the coast and find our way back to base visually. This was a sound plan, we had the skills and capability to do it and although it wasn't a cleared procedure it was one that I had practiced in the simulator many times. However, it was always emphasized to me by the simulator instructors that this was an emergency let down procedure. So, I reckoned we were in an emergency. I quickly plotted our planned routing onto a chart and programmed the RNS 252. The AWACS would be able to give us a rough location of where we were from their radar signature, but we would have to allow for a lot of error as this was not precise navigation. I prepared to speak to the AWACS operator to outline what we wanted to do and what help we wanted from them when 'dink' – the navigation systems all came back on line. "What happened there?" I asked. "I dunno – but we seem to have our nav kit back." replied Jim. I dialed in the details for Split Airport's navigation beacon and rightly enough the pointer responded and the beacon coded correctly. We verified the codes and we were able to adjust our route and head for the airport. Half an hour later we made a sound ILS approach through cloud and safely onto the runway. We hover taxied along the runway and hopped across to Divulje Barracks where we landed, closed down and were met by our engineers who would put the aircraft to bed. It had been a long night, and I was tired. We had a quick debrief as a crew and acknowledged a job well done. We checked that there was no other tasking that had come in and then we headed for our beds.

We had no idea what happened technically to the aircraft that night. I spoke to Jim years after the event and he had no idea what caused it. We spoke with the staff at the simulator who tried to replicate the conditions but without success. However, with hindsight I now realise that I had experienced an early, important leadership lesson. Think differently. We live in a world of norms and procedures. We expect things to work and to happen in a certain way. In the military I was trained extensively in procedures and drills and what to do when certain things do or don't happen. But on that evening in January 1996 I learnt the importance of being able to think differently in unprecedented conditions to achieve the mission.

* * *

There is something of a paradox in the military – personnel are trained to very high standards in drills and procedures with significant levels of discipline. This is understandably a sound approach as a way to be able to control groups of people and to set clear expectations. However, when things go wrong – and they do – the rehearsed drills and procedures may not always be the way forward. Personnel may need to abandon what is comfortable and familiar and instead disrupt their thinking to find another way to achieve the mission. In Bosnia for me this meant executing a procedure that was technically 'not legal' but nevertheless familiar and practiced; in Kosovo this meant working around the rules to achieve all of the tasking for a greater good. I am very fond of the phrase *"First break all the rules"* from the work by Marcus Buckingham and Curt Coffman describing what great managers do differently. I don't consider myself rebellious or unconventional or a deliberate rule-breaker; rather, this phrase *"First break all the rules"* reminds me to think differently and makes me challenge what I am assuming in any given scenario. My training to be a leadership coach has made me aware of how limited people's thinking can be because of the assumptions they are making – either explicitly or implicitly.

So, this is the second of my key leadership principles – think differently. It's near impossible to think differently if we do not have capacity to do so, hence the importance of making capacity in our lives. And of course, we may need to think differently to create capacity in the first place. Having made capacity, we are able to assess the situation - the big picture - and we have a choice: are we happy with the status quo or is change needed? Maintaining the status quo is a management exercise – ensuring supply meets demand, resources are supported etc. However, if the status quo is not satisfactory, or more likely in the current age unsustainable, then leadership is required. And the responsibility of the leader is to think differently about how to achieve the same or better results.

Adversity forges leadership, along with character and affinity and *esprit de corps* in teams. Of course, it is not ethical to prescribe adversity – the nearest the military come to this is through adventurous training and survival training – placing people in difficult situations physically, mentally and emotionally and seeing how they respond. Unfortunately, in many corporate settings that I have witnessed the adversity comes about through change due to restructures and downsizing, often reactively through a failure to adapt to a changing context sooner. Although there is an inevitability to the change required, it is feared and resisted because it is uncomfortable and uncertain. Leaders often do not make sufficient capacity to think about and articulate how the landscape needs to be different and so the whole process becomes slow and painful. Leaders who think differently early on can visualise the new world and see past the present pain. Through humility, courage, determination and usually some exquisite communications and planning they are able to take their people – most if not all of them - to the new destination in a more efficient and empowering way.

My environment on that night in Bosnia was already a stressful one: operationally pressured, demanding flying conditions and high levels of expectation – not to mention it was my first operational deployment as a navigator. However, I had the training to equip me for the situation and I was part of the best team I could have hoped to be with. Despite the conditions though, an unprecedented event still happened. So, in your own situation I wonder:

- Are you facing challenging circumstances?
- Do you have the high performing team you would like around you?
- Do you have the competence and capability to do what you anticipate needs doing?

As well as all of these factors, as the leader you need to be ready to think differently and stay ahead of the situation before your time and your fuel runs out.

Questions from your navigator:

- Does something need to change?
- Are there areas for you that aren't working as they should be?
- What routines or habits are you in – and do they serve your mission?
- Who can help you to look at things differently…someone to disrupt your thinking as a catalyst to change?

EMPOWERMENT

'I've learned that people will forget what you said, people will forget what you did, but people will never forget how you made them feel.'
—**Maya Angelou**

"You can do what I cannot do. I can do what you cannot do. Together we can do great things."
—**Mother Teresa**

'Leaders become great, not because of their power, but because of their ability to empower others."
—**John Maxwell**

For several months, a project team had been working on a new Initial Officer Training Course (IOTC) at Royal Air Force College Cranwell's Officer and Aircrew Cadet Training Unit. Originally the IOTC was 18 weeks; this had increased to 24 weeks when I joined the Royal Air Force in 1992 and the course was being reviewed again in 2005 with a view to structuring the training over three terms to align it with officer training in the other two armed services, namely Britannia Royal Naval College, Dartmouth, for the Royal Navy and Royal Military Academy, Sandhurst for the Army. In 2005 I led Training Standards (TS); four officers charged with training the Flight Commanders (Flt Cdrs) who in turn would train the Officer Cadets embarking on a career in the Royal Air Force as commissioned officers. This was on the back of spending two years training officers on the main IOTC Squadrons, one of the most fulfilling jobs I have ever undertaken. This gave me a thorough understanding of the syllabus and more importantly how to develop and assess young leaders.

Part of the work of refreshing the IOTC was to make it more relevant to modern day situations. Several new exercises had been designed for the field leadership training phase which was where leadership tasks were undertaken by officer cadets and assessed in outdoor training areas, usually military ranges in Norfolk or Northumbria. The tasks had evolved from the challenge of getting the team across an obstacle area of proverbial shark infested custard to more realistic challenges of environmental incidents and Military Aid to the Civil Powers (MACP). It was during the trialling and testing of one of these new exercises that I had the epiphany of leadership being about truly *empowering* followers.

The TS team had found time between the routine programmes of training Flt Cdrs and assessing them with their cadets, where we could travel to one of the training areas and test some of the new tasks that had been designed. The four of us in TS travelled to Thetford in Norfolk where we would spend three days working and testing the new exercises. To help us, we had some cadets from MASH – Medical and Special Holding Flight. These were cadets who had started training but for one reason or another had their training suspended. Often this was due to injury but could also be for compassionate reasons; basically, the cadets on MASH were 'holding' for a date when they could recommence their officer training. For our purposes these cadets would be our guinea pigs…they knew enough of the system to be able to conduct themselves with military bearing and any training they could get would help them stay engaged whilst they were holding. The opportunity to get out onto a training area and be exposed to new exercises was actually in some ways an advantage for them as it offered a potential sneak preview to training that they would in due course undertake when they themselves would be assessed for their suitability to be awarded a Queen's Commission. It was also an opportunity for them to exercise and practice their own personal leadership qualities and receive feedback from seasoned Flt Cdrs.

We had eight cadets with us who would replicate a flight of cadets that a regular Flt Cdr would be responsible for training on the IOTC; a flight was usually ten to twelve cadets. Our colleagues in the course design team had prepared a new exercise along the theme of MACP. The brief was that there had been an industrial incident which had resulted in toxic chemicals being released into a local water course and the contamination was flowing towards a main river. The task was to arrange a barrier across the tributary to contain the spillage so that specialist teams could be brought in to collect and dispose of the contaminants. The exercise would require an appreciation and understanding of the problem, planning and organisation of how to implement a solution, effective communication to the team and decision making as the situation unfolded. These were some of the nine Personal Leadership Qualities or PLQs that the cadets were continuously assessed against. In later years these PLQs evolved into 9 Leadership Attributes[17].

For this exercise I had Officer Cadet Graves as my lead and I would be in the role of the Flt Cdr. Graves was typical of the fantastic raw

---

[17] 1. war fighter courageous 2. emotionally intelligent 3. willing to take risks 4. flexible and responsive 5. able to handle ambiguity 6. technologically competent 7. able to lead tomorrow's recruit 8. mentally agile and physically robust 9. politically and globally astute – air power minded

material that we had to work with as Flt Cdrs - a female graduate twenty something who was physically fit, ambitious and keen to learn; smart in appearance and engaging to work with. The day would start with an inspection of the flight that ensured that the cadets were practically prepared for the day, for instance that they had the correct personal equipment for the conditions. This lite ceremony also reinforced preparation for Service life where discipline and procedures were important and needed to be respected. Following the inspection of the whole Flt the standard protocol was to take the cadet lead to one side and brief them on the mission, check their understanding of the task and give them time to come up with a plan. The cadet would then brief their plan back to the Flt Cdr before going to brief their team and getting on with the task. On this particular occasion we had some senior officers in attendance from the College who were keen to see how the new course design was progressing. Essentially, they were there to watch me and understand how the Flt Cdrs would be expected to conduct the new training.

Earlier in the year IOTC Flt Cdrs had attended a Transactional Analysis 101 course, organised by the TS team. I had come to realise that the protocol of getting the cadet leader to brief the Flt Cdr on their solution was actually quite controlling and drove a parent-child dynamic in the relationship. Essentially, the Flt Cdr was giving the cadet leader permission to carry out their plan. Whilst this made for the smooth running of an exercise in a limited time frame, I was curious about how much of the task was actually owned by the cadet leader and how much was being controlled by the Flt Cdr. So here I was in a unique opportunity; we were trialling a leadership task, the cadet lead was not being formally assessed, so the outcome would not impact on their success at IOT. So the whole episode was consequence free but ripe for learning. After the requisite five minutes for planning time had elapsed Graves came up to me with her well drilled and expected narrative:

"Sir, I've come up with a plan and I'm ready to share this with you." Usually the Flt Cdr would listen, give their approval (permission) or not to proceed, maybe offering a few suggestions, and the cadet lead would then get on with it.

"Ok Graves, what have you got." I asked. Graves explained to me what her understanding of the problem was and how she proposed to address the situation with the resources at her disposal. The main issue to the challenge was how to get across the tributary so that a boom could be positioned across the water course in order to contain the contamination that was heading that way.

Usually after the cadet lead's short briefing to the Flt Cdr, the Flt Cdr would be expected to ask a couple of probing questions and then tell the cadet to get on with it. Whilst Graves had been planning and subsequently briefing me, her team had been sat around waiting, enjoying some warm spring sunshine before they were required to get working and start moving equipment to get the task done. For some reason I was in a playfully cantankerous mood that day. Graves finished her briefing to me and there was a pause. She was expecting me to say:

"Very good Graves, a couple of questions…" and then proceed with the task. However, feeling playful I challenged her:

"Is that it?" I asked, with a marginally sarcastic tone. "Is that all you've come up with?"

Graves physically rocked back on her boots

"Err…Sir?"

"How many ideas have you come up with?" I inquired.

"Two or three…I think I've picked the best one." Graves replied, almost apologetically and with a little nervousness.

"Yes, you've come up with two or three – and your team has done what in that time?" I asked rhetorically.

"How many ideas to solve this task could you have come up with?" Graves was starting to get it; her face was turning from nervous confusion to anticipation.

"You mean, Sir, if I had engaged with my team in my planning just now…?"

"Precisely, if you've come up with two or three ideas, how many could eight of you come up with…and which one of those ideas would be the best?"

I could see that Graves had had the realisation of what I was alluding to and she was wanting to get back to her team to engage them in the task. There was no shame in what she had done. All cadets were conditioned to take the brief, come up with a plan, their plan, and then check that plan with the Flt Cdr. After all, much of military life is about routine drills and procedures that usually exist for good reasons. However, I realised this was such a limited use of the resource available, namely the team, and more importantly set up a poor leadership practice at the start of these young officers' leadership careers. Of course, it was important that junior officers were capable of understanding the problem and coming up with a solution - and this aspect of training was not to be ignored. However, there was a dearth of development around how to engage, collaborate, and utilise a team to get the optimum result.

As always time was limited – but on this occasion I had the luxury of controlling the timeline.

"Graves, I'm going to give you five minutes with your team, and I want you to see how many ideas you can come up with to solve this problem. *Go.*" Graves saluted me, I returned the compliment, and she then dashed over to her team who by now had detected that things weren't going 'as normal' and they looked agitated. Graves got stuck into briefing them on the task and our abnormal conversation and subsequently got the team brainstorming. I turned around to my colleagues and senior visitors who had been standing within earshot but at an appropriate distance.

"That was different" Matt said, my closest friend on TS. The senior leaders looked somewhat bewildered – this wasn't what they were used to seeing but they liked the energy they could see among Graves and her team.

"Right Graves, that's five minutes. Come over here. How many solutions have you got?" I asked.

"Thirty Sir." Graves remarked, proudly.

"And which one of those thirty is the best one?" I asked.

"This one Sir." Graves showed me a schematic plan in her field notebook of how they would get across the tributary and construct the floating barrier.

"Whose idea was that?" I asked.

"Jenkins' Sir."

"So, you're going with an idea that wasn't your own?"

"Yes Sir – is that alright?" I noticed her desire to still seek approval.

"What are you asking me for? It's your lead. Get cracking and we'll see how it goes." By this stage Graves had sussed me out – I was not a hard-nosed Flt Cdr looking to score points on her to stroke my own ego in front of senior officers or peers. Rather, I was someone who was focussed on her development, albeit with an unconventional and unorthodox approach. What astounded me was the change in energy in Graves' fellow cadets. From a bunch of people who had been laying in the sun waiting for things to start and being told what to do by a fellow cadet, who quite frankly they may not have actually liked or respected, they had transformed into a focussed group keen to contribute and get things moving. Because Graves had engaged them from the start and opted to use an idea that came from the team, everybody seemed to be owning the solution rather than grudgingly going through the motions until it was 'their' turn to lead.

The duration of the whole exercise lead was three hours and at the end of the exercise the team of cadets along with the Flt Cdrs present had the customary huddle and debrief of what had happened to extract learning. The task had been a success.

"What did you learn from that Graves?" I asked.

"That I'll always have ideas for how to solve a problem; but the best idea may not be my own and as leader it's ok for me to make sure the best possible idea available is used. And I'm still responsible for seeing the task completed."

The senior observers looked impressed. We had just realised that it was possible to equip leaders with a mind-set of empowerment that did not detract from their authority as leader. The leader did not need to have all of the answers – sometimes they don't need any of the answers. The leader needed to be able to understand where the best competence was, how to access it and use it to achieve their mission. The by-product of engaging the team in this process was increased morale and ownership by the team. And I noted to myself that the core quality of the leader in this situation was humility - the need to think about others rather than only thinking about them self.

Within months of this event my tour at IOT had come to a close and I was posted to my next role – sadly before the course review had been completed and before I could see Graves re-join a main squadron and complete her officer training. I was unable to see the finished product. However, my colleague Matt relayed to me some months later that when the new training leads were rolled out and the exercise referenced above was delivered as part of the mainstream programme, Flt Cdrs used exactly the same dialogue, almost word for word, that I had used with Graves – I like to think with similarly cantankerous mischievousness. Furthermore, several years later I was meeting with a new friend from the Centre for Leadership Studies at Exeter University – himself and ex-Royal Marine - and sharing stories from the leadership development aspects of our respective military careers.

"Were you at RAF College Cranwell around the time when they started delivering a truly empowered model of leadership?" I was dumbfounded. My cantankerous challenge to Graves on that warm spring morning several years earlier had disrupted the status quo of training that was delivered and left a legacy that transformed the approach to leadership development at a premier military academy.

* * *

The truth is that on that day in Thetford in Norfolk I had an idea of how to solve the problem that I had given to Graves; in fact, as a Flt Cdr I had the 'blueprint' for how the lead *should* be done. I could have cajoled and controlled Graves towards the solution that I wanted to see, either for her success or for my ego, but this wouldn't have used any of her personal power and certainly wouldn't have utilised the potential within the team. The beauty of this episode for me was that, albeit with an unconventional approach, I unconsciously gave Graves the permission to use her own personal power and authority to do something in her own way. In turn, she gave power to the team to come up with the optimal solution – she empowered them.

There seems to be a reluctance in this post austerity age for leaders to give power to others, perhaps in case they are perceived as incapable themselves and consequently susceptible to 're-structures'. The relentless pursuit of busyness means that leaders need to own more tasks and issues and problems as if this somehow enhances their identity as a leader. With this approach power creeps up the hierarchy with the consequence that less peoples' brains are engaged in solving problems. So the scope and arguably the quality of problem solving is reduced. And a consequence of this is that less people are engaged with the process and correspondingly staff engagement and morale suffer. To give power to others – to empower them – requires a degree of vulnerability on the part of the leader. The leader has to trust their people, and this may well require courage.

There was a cynical saying we had in the Royal Air Force that was "Knowledge is power, and knowledge shared is power halved." This attitude betrays a defensive stance, one that is fearful of other people presenting solutions with your information; possibly solutions that may be better than what you could have come up with. I believe that in fact if power can be distributed within a team or even an organisation then the best possible performance can be realised by those best equipped to deliver it. This was evident to me on my check ride to become a Mission Commander, described in the next chapter. I could not possibly know the full capability of all of the assets under my command, I had to delegate and trust that the team members were competent and motivated to make their own, specific contributions. Part of the definition of empowerment is *"the process of becoming stronger and more confident"*. What sound and rational leader would not want their organisation to become stronger and more confident?

Why is this so important to me? I have an ideological if not naïve philosophy that in a part of the world there may be a child living in poverty who may not see their fifth birthday because of disease or malnutrition. But if they were given the opportunity to exercise their personal power and realise their full potential, then just maybe they could make a contribution and perhaps even discover something phenomenal; like a cure for cancer or a solution to global poverty. They could certainly make a meaningful contribution to the world. However, they may never get the opportunity. The world needs great leaders who can empower others in order to realise the full potential of our fellow humans. Empowerment leads to engagement, motivation, solutions, innovation, ideas, resourcefulness, collaboration, growth. To do this the leader needs to engage with others, and the leader needs to demonstrate humility and courage in doing so.

Questions from your navigator:

- Who could contribute more than you're presently allowing them to do?
- What would it take for you to give some of your 'personal power' to them?
- What if their solution is better than the one you could come up with?

MISSION COMMAND

"I make known the end from the beginning."
—Isaiah 46:10

"Before we start, what sort of day are we going to have? This is my Mission Command lead and I don't want to see it derailed by shoddy time-keeping. Is that understood? If we say that the brief starts at 0800, it starts at 0800…ok?"

It was 10th August 2000 and I was addressing the senior officers and instructors of the Rotary Wing Operational Evaluation Training Unit, and my fellow students of No. 15 Qualified Helicopter Tactics Instructor Course (QHTIC) at Royal Air Force Leeming in Yorkshire. This was my check ride; I had to pass the day to become a Qualified Helicopter Tactics Instructor (QHTI); one of the most coveted qualifications to hold on a Support Helicopter (SH) Squadron - and I was starting the day by giving a bollocking!

I had been getting frustrated. From my early days in the Royal Air Force, like everyone else in the room, I had been taught to always be five minutes early. Much of life in the military revolves around briefings and punctuality, to a degree this was part of our professionalism and what the military is known for. Ultimately, operationally, there was little room for error with timings. Being late or early could have life threatening consequences. I had noticed that during the week, staff, and some students, had got into the habit of arriving for briefings just in time, or maybe not, and certainly not respecting the five minutes before rule. Since the briefing started with a time check it was essential that everyone was present and ready to synchronise watches so that we would all be on the same time throughout the mission. I wanted to set a standard and assert my authority on the day so that everyone knew that I was the Mission Commander (MC) that day and that it mattered.

I was getting an enthusiastic thumbs up and silent 'yeeessss Rich' from Paul, our lead crewman, sitting several rows back in the briefing room. He and the other crews had been dutifully waiting on time in the briefing room; equally frustrated as me that the front row occupants were dragging their heels. I had been in work from 0630hrs, which was when I received the met brief for the day and the frag sheet, the detailed mission instruction that I was responsible for planning and leading throughout day. The mission started proper for all participants with the time check and main briefing at 0800hrs. There then followed about five hours of planning followed by a three-hour flying mission. When we landed there would be a series of debriefings. It would be a long day. The spotlight was on me and this day was important to me. So, to have the front row of my briefing walk in with plus or minus seconds to spare was not good enough; we needed to be clear on what sort of standards we would keep for the day. I think I gave two bollockings in my sixteen-year Royal Air Force career; this was the first one. To be fair, the culprits on the front row looked suitably awkward, embarrassed and penitent and so we got on with the show. Despite being junior in rank to several of the people on the front row, my authority as MC was established.

The mission was, as it often was for SH mission leads, to pick up some troops from somewhere and then insert them somewhere else tactically as part of a war game scenario. Along the way we would face various threats from the ground and the air – different military assets that would be trying to shoot us down. This would include radar guided missile systems from ground units, radar missiles, infra-red missiles and cannon guns from role playing enemy fighter aircraft. We would need to deploy our tactics to defeat the threats and achieve the mission. As Mission Commander, I had to conduct the whole piece. At my disposal were multiple blue air assets, meaning friendlies, such as other SH units, fast jets, radar jammers and AWACS. Attempting to defeat my mission there was red air – simulated enemy players within the 'game' who would know an appropriate amount of our plans so that they could ambush us and test our tactics. It wouldn't be much of an assessment of our tactical ability if we totally evaded the enemy for the whole sortie, although of course that is what we would be aiming for in real life.

My mission brief was a standardised format that addressed all aspects of the sortie and took up several pages of an A4 book known as the 'blue brain'. It was called this as it contained all of the supplementary information that I may need to call on whilst airborne, and accordingly it was carried in a pouch next to my seat in the Chinook's cockpit. Several pages may sound a lot but most of it was routine drills familiar to the crews who were, frankly, at the top of their game to even be taking part in the QHTIC. I delivered the mission brief that detailed various duties to various elements and confirmed key timing events. A lot of detailed planning and briefing would be done separately by the specific aircraft types crews taking part. However, it was essential that everyone was on the same page from the start; everyone knew what the mission was; everyone knew what they had to do and who else was doing what.

When the briefing was over, the respective elements dispersed to their individual planning areas within the hangar and I had an overwhelming sense of peace at a job well done – albeit only the first five per cent of the mission maybe. This lasted about a nanosecond, after which I was flooded with thoughts of 'what ifs' i.e. what if this went wrong or that didn't work? By delivering a clear and well thought through master brief I had created for myself some *capacity*…affording me the breathing space and head space to entertain the 'what ifs' and if necessary, think differently through how respective contingencies would play out. Sure enough, over the next few hours of planning the different element leads would come to me at different times with their concerns:

"Rich, we only have three out of four jets serviceable" my blue air lead advised me at one point.

"Ok, how many do you think we need?" I asked. I had already reckoned in my contingency thinking that two was a minimum and therefore that would be the 'no go' call.

"We need a minimum of two to give the package cover." he declared.

"Ok, so we can go with three. Let's carry on." I said.

One of the protocols I loved about the MC role was how he or she occupied a preserved, physical space in the flight planning area. The idea of this was to preserve the MC's capacity and keep them from distractions. It would have been very comfortable for me to spend the planning time with my SH colleagues, overseeing their route planning and even getting involved myself. After all, this was my comfort zone. However, throughout the planning phase I maintained my distance so that I could oversee the big picture and ensure the whole was coming together well. I routinely 'toured' the different planning areas to monitor progress and check in with my section leads. The people now working hard to implement the plan that I had briefed earlier were experts in their fields – trained and competent pilots, navigators and crewmen who knew what they had to do. What they didn't know perhaps as well as me was the big picture and how it was all coming together. That was my job. Keeping oversight of everything without being sucked into detail allowed me to keep a suitably critical analysis of progress. In addition to my preserved space, which would be indicated by tape on the floor, I would have a dedicated floor-walker; someone I trusted who fielded inputs to the MC so that I didn't become overwhelmed or distracted with unnecessary detail. No-one could cross into the taped area to speak to the MC without the floor walkers say so. All together this protocol ensured that my capacity was preserved.

The need to preserve my capacity to be able to monitor the big picture continued into the air. The temptation when being the MC is to sit in the front seat of the lead helicopter, able to control and direct progress. However, being an active operator would leach my capacity and absorb me in detail – especially during mission critical episodes – the very times when I needed to be scanning the big picture for overall mission success. The ideal location for a MC would be aboard the AWACS. Having full sight and sound of mission progress from a relatively safe vantage point. However, this was not logistically possible for my lead. There were three Chinooks in our formation, and each had a 'jump seat' – a collapsible seat between the pilot and navigator in the cockpit with access to all of the communications available. Therefore, I claimed the 'jump seat' on the third Chinook for myself for when we were airborne. I trusted my SH colleagues to lead this formation and follow the plan. My role was to monitor and observe, ready to intervene with MC authority if a mission critical decision was required. If I needed to do this, I had a personal call sign to use so that everyone knew it was me calling the shots.

The jump seat was familiarly known as the capacity seat. From this vantage point in the cockpit, where performing operational duties was limited, it was still possible to see, and hear, everything. Often passengers who were being given a 'familiarisation sortie' or what we perhaps better knew as a 'joy ride', would sit in the jump seat to experience flying in a Chinook, but possibly be unaware of what was going on. In other contexts, instructors would sit in the jump seat to monitor and assess a crew's performance on a check ride or training sortie. From an operational perspective, the jump seat gave the occupant a great 'big picture' of progress without getting distractingly drawn into operating the platform they were sat on - the two front seat occupants could be trusted to do that, that was their job.

By early afternoon the planning cycle was complete. As MC, I led the overall mission brief before respective sections split to conduct their specific pre-flight briefings. It was a warm summer's day and we were blessed with a great forecast that would allow all aspects of the assessment to take place. The cloud base and visibility were such that the enemy fighters would be able to find us and engage with us, ensuring that the tactics of evading enemy aircraft could be tested. We walked to the aircraft, carried out an exquisite start up, taxi and take-off as a formation and executed a successful mission. We were engaged by surface to air missile systems, we had our communications intercepted and jammed, and were attacked by 'red-air' fighters who attempted to shoot us down with radar and infra-red missiles and close quarter cannon fire. We deployed our tactics effectively and achieved the mission. I had passed my check ride as a mission commander and was subsequently awarded my QHTI badge – which I wore with pride for another three years on the Squadron and beyond in subsequent tours of duty. The skills I had learned in my training would serve me well in the coming years when I was selected to be in the lead crew that invaded Afghanistan. As important, I had learnt several key leadership principles: the importance of having a clarity of purpose on any endeavour by defining the **mission**; preserving my **capacity** to optimise my awareness of the big picture; and when necessary to **think differently** about how to resolve emergent issues. Through all of these I recognised the importance of utilising the significant talent of the whole team to achieve the mission through **empowerment**, giving people who were really good at doing their job the space to perform brilliantly.

Many years later, after I had left the RAF, a good friend and colleague of mine who had been part of the Directing Staff that day remarked to me that the RWOETU team agreed that my check ride was the best Mission Command lead they had seen. I was never told.

* * *

Mission Command is a huge concept in its own right and the language can make it appear an exclusively military phenomenon. In the Royal Air Force we regularly flew *missions* and when these escalated in scale from single aircraft sorties to multiple aircraft deployments during large scale operations then a sophisticated and effective command and control structure was required. However, it is easy to forget that at the heart of missions – and arguably their success or failure – is the human element. People, with all of their emotions, uncertainties, and varying levels of confidence, competence and motivation, are often the determining factor in whether a mission is successful or not. Most people want to do a good job, and with a little encouragement, training and inspiration they can be capable of great things. Leaders forget this at their peril in environments where the seduction of impersonal and automated processes can take over. People matter, and people are what make a difference. They can be scared, inefficient and dis-engaged...or they can be courageous, innovative and passionate. It often comes down to how they are led. In describing mission command Stephen Bungay says:

> *"Battlefield success depended on incisive leadership and a sense of personal responsibility for achieving collective outcomes. Senior people had to articulate their intent, give clear briefings, and leave well alone. Junior people had to understand the intent, appraise their own situation, and make rapid decisions to realise it based on partial information."*
> **—Stephen Bungay; Sandhurst Foundation Newsletter, November 2010**

From this description there are some key elements: intent, clarity, sensemaking and responsibility for action. In my own experience I have distilled Mission Command down to three main points which I believe are transferable and valid in any organisational context.

- What is the Commander's Intent? (Purpose – start with why)
- What resources do I have?
- Do I have any questions?

Commander's Intent. Contextually in the military this would be the intent of the commander two levels up from the leader's position. What do they actually want to achieve and what is the outcome? The overall objective of a war may be to defeat the Taliban and end global terror attacks – but this is a big and complex task. I would need to know what my part in that overall objective was. So, for example, the intent would be to have Royal Air Force Chinooks based in Bagram that could be used to deploy troops in that country. In other words, we can refer to this as *purpose*. And the more clarity there is around the purpose the more accurately success can be measured. The outcome was to have two Chinooks deployed to Bagram ready for operational tasking on 26th March 2002. We achieved the mission, or at least our part of it. I needed to understand the big picture, the overall objectives and within them, what my contribution was to be.

In your organisation the same is true – do you know what your overall purpose is? And do you know what your contribution is to achieving that purpose? Many organisations fail to have a really clear mission that translates to and engages with everybody as part of the beating rhythm of their daily reality. It is achievable, and it can be simple, and it needs the leader to communicate it, believe it and live it – evidenced through their behaviours. When this happens, people can invest themselves into the cause and great things can be achieved.

> *"Clarity of mission builds unity."*
> **—Nehemiah 3 v 17-18**

Resources. You will never have as much resource as you want to get the job done. I have yet to work in a setting where the organisation could say *"we're good for resources thanks…do you want some back?"* I'm talking about people, money and time. During my own Initial Officer Training I listened to a talk of how the Royal Air Force was ill-equipped and under-manned to face the growing threats on the world stage of increasingly political uncertainties. There were not enough pilots, not enough planes and not enough time to train more pilots. This made sense to me; it was 1992, the Cold War had recently 'finished', and we were responding to a Strategic Defence Review which was of course an opportunity to reduce defence spending. The result? Not enough people or time and the wrong equipment to face the emerging and uncertain threat. However, having spelt out a context that was real time familiar, the speaker then indicated that he was reflecting a report that was written in 1938. A lack of resource would appear to be a constant and universal complaint.

But with resources this is the point. We never have enough, and we often don't have what we would like. But do we actually know what we do have at our disposal? If we are clear about what we have then we can crack on with finding a way to achieve the mission. This drives innovation if we harness thinking differently. History, in particular wars, are littered with examples of innovation through adversity. People making do with what they had to get the job done. Or better still, finding new ways of doing old things. I have worked in several public-sector organisations over the past decade that have been responding to the ravages of austerity following the financial crash of 2008. It may be too early to see what the long-term effects will be – but many organisations have found new efficiencies through adversity and are delivering unforetold benefits. For sure, in some cases the cuts may have gone too far. But there is still learning to be had there. If the Royal Air Force had had 'enough' Spitfires in 1940, and how many would 'enough' have been, then would we have developed RADAR? Would we have nurtured a flexible and responsive way to deploy limited resources to where the need was greatest, effectively? Be clear on what you do have and start thinking now about how you can use that to achieve your mission, rather than lamenting 'lack'.

Questions. The third principle in my understanding of mission command is asking questions. If I'm clear on the intent and I know what resources I have then there shouldn't be any questions. If I'm not entirely clear on 'why' I'm doing what I'm doing, then I need to check my understanding. If I'm not clear on what resources I have at my disposal then I need to check my understanding. If I've got a lot to do, then I need to prioritise. If there are a lot of questions remaining, then this may be to do with the clarity and communication with which the mission was briefed in the first place. However, this does not excuse me taking responsibility to seek the clarification I need.

In simple terms this is the contract between you and your leader. I suppose what often derails this contract is a lack of true empowerment. Leaders can ask their people to do things but then do not give them the proper authority and control at the appropriate level. This may be a trust issue. Do I trust my people to do what I 'commanded' and with that give them permission to be innovative and resourceful in getting the job done? Or do my insecurities inhibit my ability to delegate control and stifle the opportunity for thinking differently. In truth, I believe people have the capacity to be brilliant. However, they are often inhibited by baggage, either their own or that of their leader. If, as a leader, I can remove the baggage then I can release potential and be surprised by brilliance. When people can connect with a purpose and be allowed to contribute their unique God-given talents, which are usually considerable, then success will follow.

During my check ride to be a QHTI I learned the need to be clear with my intentions, to work with the resources I had and to be available to my team. This required me to always have capacity and to be ready to think differently, or allow others to think differently, to solve the challenges we were presented with. As a result, the wider team were empowered, they contributed, and the mission was achieved.

Questions from your navigator:

- What is your purpose?
- How clear is your intent?
- What resources do you have?
- What questions need to be answered so that you can crack on?

CONCLUSION

"If you don't know where you're going, any path will take you there."
—Lewis Carroll

2008 was the year I left the Royal Air Force, and it was also when I completed my sponsored Masters in Research in Leadership Studies at Exeter University. Towards the end of the course my tutor gave me some feedback:

"Rich, you're not an academic; you're a practitioner."

Initially I was mortified. Here was my tutor, my academic mentor and a source of affirmation on the course telling me that I was not an academic whilst I was studying at a leading British University. For most of the 2-year course I had envied a fellow student who had consistently scored in the high nineties percentages with her assignments and was being encouraged to publish her work – and my tutors feedback made me feel, momentarily, like I was failing. But then I realised that my tutor was not insulting me or intending me harm. He saw my true identity – someone who was a practitioner in leadership, able to equip and support leaders on their journeys.

If I was an academic, then this book would be pre-occupied with an argument or arguments to convince you that my findings were provable and sound based on large amounts of qualitative and/or quantitative research. It would probably also be a lot longer for you to read! Instead, I have shared with you what I know from my own experience works with leadership. Notwithstanding the value I place on academics and their research, I am thankful that I am a practitioner. I am an award-winning navigator and mission commander of Royal Air Force pedigree who has progressed to become a navigator for leaders and leadership. My insightful analysis of a situation readily identifies the skills and qualities required to reach a performance solution and I provide the architecture to address the challenge. In essence, I work with people, teams and organisations to get them from A to B.

I have shared with you some of my experiences that have led me to conclude that the three most important leadership qualities are humility, courage and determination. I have also shared four leadership principles that are definitely effective in improving performance: making capacity, thinking differently, empowerment and mission command. My experiences in my early military career and latterly working in the corporate landscape have forged my conclusions. However much the context shifts, each of these traits will be found in some form where great leadership is taking place.

Therefore, I have distilled the learnings that I have articulated in this book into a pragmatic programme to support and equip leaders in their contexts. I have called this the Navigator Programme. If the end of chapter questions have provoked you to consider how your own leadership context could be improved then the Navigator Programme is for you.

The Navigator Programme is not solely a technical solution, it is an adaptive problem-solving mindset. The Navigator Programme is the product of my experience and the traits described in this book. The Navigator Programme is a journey, with a map, that reflects five stages that any leadership endeavour includes – whether it is for you as an individual, your leadership team or the whole organisation. These five stages are Mission, Sense-making, Plan, Deliver, Assess.

The first step on the Navigator Programme journey is to articulate the **mission** – to start with 'why' and to be clear on the purpose of the journey. As a navigator in the Royal Air Force, without a destination clearly defined it was pointless, and a waste of resources, to get airborne. This doesn't mean the destination can't change, sometimes this will happen en-route; but it is necessary to know where you intend going from the outset. In the same way any leadership endeavour needs to know where it is going – primarily to give the right sense of direction from the outset and importantly so that you can recognise when you've arrived, and you can assess the journey. Then follows what can be the most important stage, but is frequently rushed or not done at all, the **sense-making** phase. This is where making capacity is imperative to explore and understand what is really going on. The aim here is to enhance self-awareness. This may relate to an individual's mindset, a team's dynamic and capability, or the adequacy of an organisation's performance. Whichever the context, there is a range of diagnostic and psychometric tools available to understand *"what's really going on here?"* Once sense-making has been done, and in practice it is an area that needs to be revisited regularly within the journey, a **plan** can be designed. Management is often about maintaining the status quo, whereas leadership is about delivering change – *if you always do what you've always done, you'll always get what you've always got*. Therefore, the key element of the plan stage is thinking differently. The Navigator Programme uses a fun and tactile process to allow innovative, creative, different thinking to be explored which can consequently contribute to the plan. It is imperative to have a plan for a journey, but it is seductive to spend too much time planning. A cliché from my military experience rings true: no plan survives first contact with the enemy. Once a plan is made it is necessary to get going and adapt it along the way as required. To do this puts us into the **deliver** stage, where invariably the context shifts and the unexpected happens. It is essential that leaders are supported during this critical phase of the Navigator Programme and this is done though coaching along with equipping the leader to deliver effectively through empowerment of others. The Navigator Programme equips leaders with the skills that ensure that they can properly empower others and deliver the mission with accountability. Finally, we come to the **assessment** stage. Reviewing the mission and revisiting diagnostics deployed at the sense-making stage allows us to assess whether it is mission accomplished. This important final stage captures the learning from the journey, celebrates success and sets leaders up for their next journey.

Many leadership programmes offer what the supplier wants to deliver, rather than what you need. Often, they are off the shelf offerings and occasionally they are a 'tick box' exercise by the organisation to fulfil a sentiment to 'do some people development' and to use up allocated budget. It is no surprise then that when there is pressure on budgets these programmes can be the first to be shelved. In my experience, it is when the mission is most critical that the navigator's skills are needed. The Navigator Programme does not set out to satisfy some training need; rather, it is designed to work the problem using proven methods to get you, your team and your organisation equipped to journey through adversity to a brilliant outcome.

So, is your personal situation, your team, or your organisation going in the right direction? Or is it stuck in an unsatisfactory status quo? Are you facing change ahead? Do you need a navigator on board for the journey to refresh thinking and chart a new course? When teams work well and when leadership happens the outcomes are measurable...the outcomes are outstanding performance, full engagement, high levels of well-being, innovation, success, brilliance.

A Chinook helicopter is approximately eighteen tonnes of twin rotor military hardware with the potential to operate anywhere in the world 24/7. Its capability is impressive and proven over many decades. When integrated into a bigger composition of multiple aircraft it becomes part of a significant force that effects strategic and tactical change. None of this can be done without the human element. I want you to consider a metaphor here. If the Chinook represents leadership, it is only any good with a pilot. The pilot represents the leader. Collaborating with other pilots becomes a force multiplier, more can be achieved together than alone. Sometimes pilots fly missions that are straightforward and routine, they may not require a navigator. Sometimes, the mission is unclear, new, scary or into the unknown. When I launched from a Royal Navy ship's deck into the black night over the Indian Ocean heading for Afghanistan; when I set off into the winter sky over Bosnia; when I got airborne to liberate Kosovo from Serbian forces – I did not know truly what to expect. But I did have a plan, some highly skilled people around me and the confidence to deal with whatever I faced with courage and determination. Sometimes it helps to have a navigator on board for the journey – suggesting a way forward, looking out for danger and making sure progress is made. If you need a navigator, if your team needs a navigator, or if your organisation needs a navigator, then I can help you.

36732565R10068

Printed in Poland
by Amazon Fulfillment
Poland Sp. z o.o., Wrocław